Please Dance at My Funeral

a celebration of life

by Judith Haynes

©2009 A Celebration of Life Publishing • Denver, Colorado

Published in USA by *A Celebration Of Life Publishing*
P. O. Box 631494, Highlands Ranch, Colorado 80163-1494
303-619-1727
contact@JudithHaynes.com

1st Edition
Judith Haynes
PLEASE DANCE AT MY FUNERAL: A Celebration Of Life

Cover: Painting by Ellen McGrath

ISBN 978-0-9844091-0-5
Library of Congress Control Number: 2010902396

For quantity orders, please email contact@JudithHaynes.com
or call 303-619-1727.

Printed in the United States
A Celebration Of Life Publishing
Denver, Colorado
www.JudithHaynes.com

"As a young mother of small children, it seems reasonable to deny that premature death could occur. This book helped me realize that, although my husband and I are young parents, no one is exempt from the possibility. Realizing now the important decisions which need discussed, I feel more knowledgeable and empowered."

Jen Noelle

"I recommend people of all ages read this book. *Please Dance At My Funeral* contains a wealth of information and wisdom. Even if someone has already made their plans, it provides a helpful check list, and possibly new information for their consideration and use."

David Ferguson

"End-of-life decisions is a topic that is important to each and every one of us. While this topic is not always easy to talk about, this book offers practical suggestions to help you speak with your loved ones on vital issues. For those who haven't given thought to such matters, this will be very enlightening. The reader will find this helpful to them, and the book could also be used in a group setting. I really liked the reminders that we need to be respectful of the elderly and those nearing the end of life."

Carolyn DeZeeuw

"The first funeral I ever attended was my husband's. We were only 31. I wore a fuchsia colored dress (his favorite) to the funeral. I know there were probably comments made, but I wanted to celebrate his life. You never know when death will affect you. We always think it is something that we don't have to think about until much later in life. This book helps to understand the emotions that accompany this very real process."

Kathy Appleton

"Having been a Hospice nurse for many years, I have cared for the dying, and for their families and friends. The book content, as well as Judith's simple, creative exercises at the end of the chapters, will be helpful to patients and their families at this sensitive time. The chapters also speak to each of us about how to live our lives more fully."

Jean Pexton

Dedication

*To my daughters, Jen and Erin, who have helped me
and tolerated my many in-depth discussions about death,
to my grandsons, Logan and Eli, who inspire me to
keep playing and living with adventure, and
to Chris, my son-in-law, to whom I am grateful
for keeping my computer functioning.
Thank you all for believing in me.
I will always love you.*

*And to my parents, Deloris and Glenn Ballard,
whose lives and deaths inspired me
to always question, to seek truth,
to communicate what was in my heart,
and to stretch my mind beyond imagined limits.*

Publisher's Note

The purpose of the *Please Dance At My Funeral* book series is to:

- challenge people to think about the final stage of their life
- educate people as to the importance of communicating about this topic
- inspire people to really identify and honor who they are
- motivate people to make decisions now about their future
- and encourage people to celebrate their life along the way

Table of Contents

Appendixes

Acknowledgments

I wish to extend my gratitude to
Trisha Hood and Jean Pexton for their continued encouragement;
to Becky Chapman and Ellen McGrath
for their patience and artistic skills;
and to Financial and Estate Planning Attorney, Jeffrey R. Young
for providing his expertise.

I also want to thank Jen, Erin, Chris, Deane, David, Carolyn
Shannon, Trisha, Kathy, Jean, and Ellen for their stories, their kind
words, their emotional support, and for sharing my vision.

As a practitioner of natural modalities, and promoting better health for nearly 30 years, I have been committed to educating my clients specifically about health issues. I am genuinely passionate about helping people, because nearly 20 years ago, a natural approach to healing saved my life.

A few years ago, I was surprised when a client spoke to me in confidence after her appointment. "My husband and I have lived our lives being so conscientious about our health, and we have taken good care of ourselves. We don't want to end up in a nursing home, or separate nursing homes. We also don't want to sit in our car in an enclosed garage with the car running, and a note to our families taped to the steering wheel! What can we do?"

Not long after, another client approached me with similar questioning. She was in her late 50s, and recently received a concerning diagnosis. I had never been asked to discuss this topic, yet it affects every single one of us.

I turned within, considered my past, and examined my own feelings about dying. My earliest memory of death was my grandfather's when I was five. I wasn't allowed to go to the funeral. It was a mystery. No one would talk to me about where he was, or why I couldn't see him again. I didn't know why everyone was crying, why people were coming to the house with food, and why everyone was dressed up. Talking about it was forbidden.

Two men taught my high school Sunday school class. Every week my hand went up again and again, wanting to discuss the lesson they had presented. Due to weariness from my questioning, I'm sure they couldn't wait for me to graduate and move out of town! When they spoke of dying I didn't agree with what they had to say. I knew there had to be a reason we come into this world. I wondered why we are here. Didn't anyone question how we could spend 24 hours a day, 8,760 hours a year, and maybe 660,000 hours in a life time just waking and working and sleeping? No one took my questions seriously. No one would discuss dying.

I was living in Connecticut when my mother died of cancer at age 65. There was no available Hospice in the area where she lived in Indiana. There was no support group for her as there are in so many areas today. On the plane to her funeral, I wrote her eulogy. We grew up attending a small Methodist church in a rural area. There were over 400 people in our little church for her funeral, and standing room only in the back. I was pregnant with my youngest daughter at the time of my mother's death. In her eulogy, I likened the dying process to the process of giving birth. One small paragraph of what I read that day is as follows:

"We enter into this world through a labor process, and we leave this world through another type of labor process, which is the spirit leaving the physical body. Yet the spirit exists, and perhaps in our dying we simply graduate to yet another phase of existence for that spirit."

After I read the eulogy, the minister rose to the microphone, cleared his throat, and said, "I don't think there is anything left to say." My father later said that in the following three weeks nearly 300 people asked for a copy of what I read. When my father died 18 years later, two ladies of our church walked up to me after the service and said they came because they thought I was going to speak again. It *wasn't* about me — it was about the *message*.

Our culture has allowed for us to view death from all negative and dark images. Words describing our engrained concepts are fear, pain, loss, and suffering. The way in which I compared the dying process to the birthing process, shed a different light to this perspective for the people attending my mother's funeral.

Death is the word that defines the ultimate experience of that which we have no knowledge or control. Unlike goal setting, we push this final stage of our life to the furthest corners of our mind, leaving the details to chance.

Have we not prepared for most other aspects of our lives in some way? If we have consciously lived our lives, can't we also consciously prepare for our leaving process as well? My mentor used to say, "Even the Saints died of something." Why do we resist talking about this life sequence that is as natural as being born? Why are we so unwilling to accept this certain progression, as if remaining in denial will prevent death, or prolong our life?

We are a culture of people, who by clutching our fear of dying, squeeze the joy out of our living. Our discomfort comes from the sense of having no control over this expected event. By living more consciously, embracing the unknown, and mentally working through the inevitable, we can diminish the fear, and live our life more fully.

A well known Buddhist nun and author, Pema Chödrön, speaks of our lives being brief, even if we live to be one hundred years old. She says, "... if you live your life as if you actually only had a day left, then the sense of impermanence heightens that feeling of preciousness and gratitude."

Would it help us to better embrace this natural progression if we speak of it now? Would our final days prove more meaningful for us if we made our wishes known, and initiated our preparations ahead of time? Would it help us to consider, as some cultures do, that it should be a time of celebration, of giving back to God—the Source of our being—that which He created?

Many years ago, a tradition was created in my family. The date of my birthday overlaps with the onset of Christmas decorations, and the playing of Christmas music. After loading Christmas music in the CD player, I encouraged my family to get up and celebrate my birthday by dancing to the song, *Linus and Lucy*, from *A Charlie Brown Christmas*. We looked silly dancing in the kitchen — and imitating Linus's dancing as shown on the TV Christmas show. We had fun.

It became a custom we have done each year on my birthday. Even if family members reside in a different city or state, we perform the tradition in unison, with phones in our hands, and the same tune playing in the background of our laughing and dancing.

After completing our dance tradition on my birthday a couple of years ago, I announced that I wanted dancing at my funeral. My family looked at me wide-eyed as if to say, *where did that come from*? I proceeded to expound on that thought, and shared with them my first vocalized wish for my end-of-life. "It should be a celebration! I want there to be a toast to my life, then I want everyone to get up and dance their hearts out to the *Linus and Lucy* song. I want you to <u>dance</u> at my funeral!"

Chapter One

"If my ship sails from sight, it doesn't mean my journey ends, it simply means the river bends." John Enoch Powell

THE CONSCIOUS JOURNEY

We learn early in our lives to set goals—learning to roll across the floor to reach a desired toy, making enough allowance to run, arms-waving, after the ice cream truck on a hot summer day, or getting into the college of our choice. Most of us have some sort of plan for each day before our feet even leave the bed, and we do so throughout the majority of our lives.

Many people think they will go along for the ride and leave to fate the final miles of their trip. Do we go to an airport, walk up to any counter, and ask to be put on any plane going anywhere? No. We plan. We visualize. We imagine what the trip will be like, and we take care of the details.

To prepare to leave this lifetime, whether it is in five months or 45 years, it behooves us to become informed. We ultimately gain in the practice of seeking greater understanding of who we are, who we have become, and how we can live in the moment with awareness.

The route of self-exploration during any stage of our life is not always common, yet it is sure to be revealing and rewarding. The means of facing truths and fears are intended to be challenging, and seeking completeness can deliver us with more freedom than we have ever before experienced.

Fear and Curiosity of the Unknown

From our first experiences and memories of death, we have emerged with curiosity and dread. In contrast to most questions we've asked our parents, answers surrounding death are either averted or vague. Generally, unless there is a death in the family, the topic might rarely be discussed between parents and children. There is often more discussion about death among teenagers due to the number of suicides and fatal auto accidents.

Distancing ourselves from death has become increasingly prevalent. The majority of people in this culture may now die in a hospital or nursing home where visitation may be restricted, and the visiting of children below a certain age prohibited. When death occurs it is neatly taken care of by the facility, and further by the call to a funeral home. This is contrasted to previous times when the body, prepared by the family, or with assistance of some fellow church members or close friends, lay in a casket in the dining room or parlor. Instead of simply attending the funeral home and funeral, families used to build the casket, dig the grave, and bury their loved one themselves — and often on their own property.

Although there are many responsibilities to consider when a family member dies, many relate now to volumes of paperwork, phone calls, and details. Many of today's tasks consist of delegation to others for transportation, providing a funeral service, or preparing a plot; then expecting substantial bills for such services. Many of these duties don't lend themselves to a time of processing and grieving. In present day, as well as years past, there is usually family and community support. However, the process of building a casket, digging a grave, or preparing a place in the home for a community viewing, may have allowed more opportunity and time for a mindfulness about the loss.

When we become intimate with the reality of dying, we can better absolve the fear, and no longer regard it as unspeakable. While dying need not be embraced until the right moment, it doesn't have to inhabit our future and consume our years with anticipated fear.

There is no way to guarantee that death won't be lonely or painful, yet until we acknowledge the inevitable, we can't enter into that state of awareness that brings completion, acceptance, and peace of heart.

When we can find it in us to be more curious than afraid,
we can piece-by-piece diminish the power we give to fear.

Sadly, Youth Are Not Exempt

If only life were so dependable that we might all assume longevity. Life doesn't come with any such guarantee. I recall a couple expecting their first child. After carrying the baby to full term, the wife learned that her baby died just one week before her due date. She still had to give birth to this baby that was no longer alive. I wondered how a heart could endure labor under such circumstances.

Another story shared with me tells of a joyous time that became a grievous occasion.

"My daughter was born needing a heart transplant. As the weeks of waiting turned into months, things often looked very bad, yet none of us dared to think anything but positive thoughts. At some point my very wise father-in-law came to us and asked the taboo and unthinkable questions: Had we thought about what we wanted if she were to die. What did we want to become of her body, and how would we want her memory to be honored.

"My husband and I could never broach the subject before because it would have seemed we were giving up her fight. My father-in-law listened to our desires with no judgment and said, 'Thank you for letting me know your wishes. We don't need to speak of this again.' When our daughter did die, he quietly took care of every detail, exactly as we had asked. We didn't even know how ill-equipped we were to handle those things at such a difficult time. I have always been so grateful for his courage to bring up the taboo subjects and force us to make sensible decisions while we could. Everyone needs someone like him to make you talk about the unpleasant subject of death, and the realities that go along with it. "

It seems that the natural order of things would allow a parent to die before a child. We can't protect them forever, and we can never know their fate. We may get used to falls, scrapes, and broken bones when they are young, but what about the number of children diagnosed early in life with threatening illnesses? What about unthinkable deaths that occur in accidents, or sports? We hold our breath as we hand our child their first set of car keys when finally of age to drive unaccompanied. We are helpless when hugging our child so tightly before they leave for active duty. If only they could all die from old age.

It is easy to imagine an average couple in their 30s or 40s with toddlers to teens all over the house, and active lives involved all over town. How many times do we hear of such a family undergoing immense stress and turmoil due to a serious diagnosis or medical condition of one of the parents? Sadly, no one is exempt from the possibility of death at any age. Accepting this fact early helps empower every parent to better plan responsibly for any possible scenario. Communicating together, making necessary decisions together, and having affairs in order, ensures a greater peace of mind should anything untimely occur.

Even the Saints Died of Something

It's natural and understandable for a patient who has just received a diagnosis of a terminal disease to demand: *Why ME? How did this happen to me? What did I do to deserve this?* When we remind ourselves that we absolutely do know that our lives will end one day, why beat ourselves up as if this is a penalty for some wrong-doing? Why waste one valuable minute imposing additional burden upon ourselves with a barrage of negative mental chatter?

How often have we acknowledged that someone we knew *lost the fight*? Well-meaning friends and loved-ones may encourage that *we can beat this thing*. Concerned physicians and caregivers may contribute words of over-optimism. Are such tactics created out of the discomfort of family, friends, and caregivers in the face of uncertainty for what lies ahead? We can participate in giving hope without postponing important conversations that need to take place.

How many times have we witnessed or heard of a patient squeezing a hand, or letting a tear roll down their cheek while confessing "I've let you down?" How can we take responsibility for disappointing our loved ones because we are experiencing this natural and final stage of our lives? We are entitled to the space of consciousness to process this immense transformation, and we look to those who are caring for us, and who love us, to stand with us through this preparation.

We have to stop thinking that a disease is a punishment or that dying is a personal failure. When we accept this fact, and release all the negative emotions tied to these beliefs, we are no longer a victim. We can instead come to a realization of empowerment. Keeping hope alive for a cure, for recovery, or for more years with a greater quality of life doesn't mean we don't need to make decisions—or communicate our wishes.

The final stage of our life should be considered as natural as birth. It is time to bring this understanding to a working concept that supports us now, even if we are young and healthy. When we reflect upon our life as a celebration of living, a celebration of accumulated wisdom and experiences, loves and relationships, we become mindful of our life in a perspective we have seldom allowed ourselves before.

For Further Contemplation

1) Close your eyes and visualize your early goals as an eight, nine or 10-year-old. See yourself as a child, remembering the satisfaction you experienced when you achieved something important to you. Now, visualize yourself as a teenager, working toward specific goals for your career or future accomplishment. See yourself entering your 20s—your 30s—and then slowly allow yourself to let your mind drift forward to the present. What do you see now?

2) Gently allow yourself to see yourself in the reality of now. Visualize caring people around you, some guiding you, and encouraging you. How does that feel? What goal comes to mind now in the midst of this visualization? Give yourself time to write some notes on what you feel and see.

Chapter Two

"Deep listening is miraculous for both listener and speaker. When someone receives us with open-hearted, non-judging, intensely interested listening, our spirits expand." Sue Patton Thoele

NO TIME FOR SILENCE

Why has it been so difficult to discuss topics surrounding death and dying? The taboo may have begun in our youth, and being hushed or given vague answers when asking about death. Often, our first experience with death has been that of a pet, and how our pet was buried or disposed of may have made a difference in our developing ideas of death.

Few may openly admit it, but harboring the belief or myth that talking about dying will expedite our death, or cause bad luck upon us or our loved ones, is a common superstition that crosses many cultures. However, keeping our thoughts to ourselves consumes more energy, and possibly hinders the situation more than when we have someone with whom to confide and share.

An elderly couple shared that they recently made all of their end-of-life decisions, and completed all of their forms and pertinent documents. They were ready to share these important decisions with their grown children, only to find that their children were not interested in going over any of this information with their parents. The plea of the couple was how to successfully initiate and create an opening for discussing this topic with their children. The suggestions in this chapter are highly recommended for improving our communication outcomes.

What is the Art of a Good Conversation? Listening!

Our inability to be a good listener inhibits the encouragement of quality communication. Yet, when conversation is easily approachable, honest, and heart-felt, the ability to openly express emotions, concerns, and decisions provides relief to family and friends.

The pivotal crux of any verbal interaction around death or dying is the need to enter into conversation with tact and great sensitivity. Even some medical professionals can fall short of having the time, or finding the most appropriate words to express genuine empathy in delivering a diagnosis or other bad news.

If there is a recent diagnosis, the need for communication and decisions are, of course, in the forefront. Extreme sensitivity is no less essential, but obvious first steps for decision making is often mandated by options presented by the physician.

When discussing important decisions, having one additional family member or person present throughout may be valuable. A third set of ears might provide more objectivity, or even encourage greater civility, during a conversation. Often it is easier for a third person to take important notes while the other two are discussing vital issues.

If there is no threat of eminent illness or death, it is more prevalent for spouses and families to put off any conversation regarding end-of-life decisions. Depending upon the way the topic is presented, a person can feel threatened and suspicious about the need to reveal intimate thoughts. Care must be given to broach the topic from either side without shutting the exchange down entirely.

My grandmother asked me to come inside when I finished mowing her lawn one day. She wanted me to pick out some dishes or furniture I would like to have after she died. Only in my teens, I was startled, and remember saying, "Oh, Grandma, you're never going to die!" In one short sentence I dismissed her wishes, denied her the gift of honoring her, and the gifts she intended to give me. This is not uncommon.

We all get into patterns of habit when it comes to speaking with family members. Over the years we create this well rehearsed tone of voice; one of protection, one of objection, one of authority, and many others. It may not seem surprising that our voice of deepest concern is often silence, either because we are afraid to voice our worries, or because we recognize the need to refrain from projecting uncertain scenarios.

When upset, worried, or nervous about discussing a topic of importance, another family member can unwittingly detect familiar tones and become unwilling to talk about a topic. Consequently, they may adopt their familiar tone of rejection back to you. Because such episodes may have become routine over the years, it is all the more important now, to increase your awareness of the tendency, and make changes.

Begin with your spouse, or a child that you often find conflict when attempting to converse. Do you dread the conversation? Is there always an initial sense of being on guard, or having to ready your defenses? Being aware of this in the forefront helps to remind your self to soften. Be quiet and listen. Genuinely hear what the other person is trying to say. Watch your temptation to respond too quickly with a familiar and patterned response. If you catch yourself wanting to respond, stop and instead nod, or say, "tell me more." Listen until you really hear and grasp what the other person is conveying. The more you become aware, and change your habits, the more you will find the conversation genuine and rewarding.

Let's look at an example:

A married couple of several years, in their 60s, have finished watching an emotion filled TV movie that left the wife solemn and wiping tears from her cheeks.

Husband: "What's the matter?"

Wife: "That show was just so true to life. It really makes you stop and think."

Husband: "It's just a movie. Pull yourself together."

Wife: "Well, think about it. That could be us! I wouldn't want to go through that the way she did in the movie! I'd want to be able to talk about it. I think we should talk about it."

Husband: "Like I said! It's just a movie. I don't need to talk about anything like that right now. I'm healthy. You're healthy. That's silly. Get over it!"

Reviewing ways in which we fall into patterns of habit, and may sabotage conversations, here are suggestions to have handled this better. First, at least the wife did express herself when asked, "What's the matter?" Many people would have responded with, "Oh, nothing," and denied their feelings. Second, it isn't acknowledging her need to express her emotions when her husband dismissed her feelings with the reply, "It's just a movie. Pull yourself together." It would have been better if he could have stopped his immediate response, and instead answered, "Maybe. Tell me more." Third, even if he didn't want to discuss the movie at that time, he might have responded by saying, "Let me think about it more."

When we tell someone, "That's silly," or other remarks that abruptly end the conversation, the person we have said this to will likely feel invalidated, and less inclined to attempt an expression of emotion in future conversations. It isn't just the tone, but the choice of words, that can essentially end a conversation before it begins.

Many people end up confiding their deepest feelings to a friend, minister, or physician, than a family member if they have not established a well-working bridge of communicating with their spouse or family. A communicating relationship is often established between people who easily empathize with a common experience, need, or story.

People who have no family, or have family members that have become estranged, may establish close bonds with friends who may become confidants, and sometimes their health advocates. People without such friends may depend more on their physicians and caregivers to supply emotional support, comfort, and be a sounding board for their concerns. This is why support groups established and offered by specific medical interest or commonalities are so valuable. Examples of these groups include: numerous Cancer support groups, those for Diabetes and Arthritis, MS, Parkinson's and Alzheimer's, Compassion and Choices, and other groups meeting various needs for specific illnesses, or for seniors.

Each recipient, in a conversation, also takes body language into consideration. The lack of eye contact, hands on the hips, or frequent glances at a watch, convey meaning. Contrast the possible subliminal meanings of those, with that of maintaining eye contact, sitting at eye level, arms uncrossed, and a smile.

If we would genuinely listen to another person, we are opening a door to encourage a two-way communication that embraces more depth of understanding.

I will probably not forget the neighbor who called two days after my miscarriage. I was, of course, still grieving my loss. She asked me how I was doing. I wasn't through the second sentence of my reply when she asked, "When is your husband coming home from work?" I was startled when she abruptly told me, "Wait and tell him," and said good-bye. We often fail to realize that as a simple sounding board we may offer the very best gift we can impart.

Check yourself before an important conversation. If you are feeling anxiety or stress, you may emanate a sense of impatience, which may prevent the other person from opening up to you.

If you are excited about something in your own life, and about to enter into a conversation with someone with whom your news would immensely contrast their state of sadness, perhaps you could first share your excitement with someone else, allowing you to be more fully present to the person you are about to visit. Be aware. Be considerate.

Take your cue from the other person. Check their body language, mood, and energy level. If your intention is to discuss serious content, and they are not feeling well that day, consider a lighter conversation, and honor their needs.

Often, comments are made which offer assumptions about the other person. "You look like you're tired? You must be feeling worse today." Instead, ask them how they are feeling and let them tell you. If you are asked for an opinion to help them make a decision, prod them with questions that help them come to their own conclusions, rather than tell them your opinion. Intently listening encourages the other person to speak more freely.

There is nothing more disheartening when confiding to someone than to have them jump in and respond with, "Oh, I know just how you feel, the other day I ...." Most of the people who say this actually have no idea how the other person is feeling, and they usually haven't listened long enough to get a real sense of what the first person is trying to share. Instead, encourage the person to really share their thoughts. If you still have something you wish to share, and genuinely can identify with what is being said, you can ensure them that you don't know *exactly* how they feel, but somewhat understand based on what they have said.

Without interrupting the speaker, encourage them to proceed with simple gestures, such as nodding your head, or simply saying, "Yes."

Remarks such as, "You shouldn't feel that way," or "What you should do is... ," diminishes the validity of the speaker's true feelings, and the ability to make their own decisions—especially if you were not asked for your opinion. Consequently, the speaker may feel that they are not entitled to the emotions that they have just confided to you.

Listeners sometimes depend on using clichés to comfort, or to create closure for the conversation in a way that appeases the visitor. A genuine hug, or squeeze of their hand, and words to let them know that you are thinking of them, might be more appropriate than expressing assurance for an outcome you have no control. If you are sincerely willing to get or do something for them, and can express your offer earnestly, it may be not only helpful for them; you may be also providing relief for their usual caregiver.

Talking to Kids

When speaking to children about illness, dying, or death, conversations which are age appropriate, and include the following, are encouraged:

1) Keep your statements of explanation simple. It is preferable to not wait or put off telling the child or children. Rather than telling them

you can't talk to them about it right now because you are too sad, spend time to respect them and their questions.

2) Answer their questions as honestly as you can. Give them time to formulate what ever they want to say. If they are young, they may immediately correlate this to taking an animal to the vet, or of a favorite pet dying. Let them speak about it in ways they understand, and be responsive to their comments in ways that keep communication open.

3) Having made your initial explanation, and having answered their initial questions, allow them time to think about what they have been told. Allow them to approach you again and again so the topic can be processed for them in their own way. If you are, in fact, not available at the moment, have your spouse or another relative fill in to provide a genuine, heart-felt exchange with the child—and then follow up, assuring them you are there, and willing to listen and talk with them.

We are so fortunate today that an awareness of how to best handle grief is extended into the schools when there has been a suicide, auto accident, illness or other trauma. Often, these are our first experiences with the grief process and experience of loss. These times are equally impactful when first occurring to us — *that could have been me, that person is my age and their life was cut short*, and an unspoken awareness — *I am mortal*. Counselors and their services are so valuable at this time, and it is also the opportunity for peer bonding around these losses that open so many doors to deep, genuine, and free expression.

A significant or first death experience for a child or teen is a vital opportunity for parents to be present—especially to listen. This is a chance to answer questions, to encourage emotional expression, and to drive them to a peer counseling, funeral, or memorial service. A parent's participation provides the opportunity for the child to witness the parent as a good listener, offering condolences and support, taking food when appropriate, and sincerely sharing in the expression of loss.

Condolences

An acquaintance once said he had been to two funerals in one week, but was unable to approach the survivors and offer condolences.

Why was that? How could this man in his 60s not have acquired the sensitivity or skill to say a kind word to the survivors of his friends? It may have been that his ability to remain stoic was dependent upon distancing himself. At a time when authentic caring is so appreciated, we all need to be able to respond to this need in an appropriate way. When you allow yourself to be vulnerable to your deepest emotions, you are in an honest place of expression to another.

The freedom to communicate openly helps meet the expressive needs of participants, while providing an opportunity for consoling in a nurturing way.

When we refuse to talk about death, we are unable to adequately prepare for the reality of all that our end-of-life experience involves. Until we renounce the denial, we refuse to let ourselves grieve, process anger, communicate to our loved ones our wishes and our love, mend the unraveling of some relationships, and come to a sense of peace of mind and heart at life's end.

For Further Contemplation

1) Practice with a friend or someone who is also willing to improve their conversational skills. First choose a common and neutral topic. With a timer set for three minutes, talk about your agreed topic, and maintain eye contact for the entire time. When the timer rings, trade places and repeat.

2) Again, with a friend or someone who is also willing to improve their skills, choose a topic between you that is more controversial. With a timer set for three minutes, talk about your agreed topic, and at the point where you would normally be tempted to interject your experience, opinion, or judgment, instead say, "tell me more," or "how do you feel about that?"

Afterwards, review with the friend the process you went through to play out these roles and what you learned about your listening skills.

Listen

Listen with your ears.
Express with your eyes.
Process and assimilate with your heart.
Acknowledge with your head.
Integrate these features
physically
emotionally
and mentally.
>>What is left out?
>>The mouth!
Too often we hear
without fully processing
and then speak before thinking.
Remember!
Sometimes speaking is not needed at all!

"A childlike man is not a man whose development has been arrested; on the contrary, he is a man who has given himself a chance of continuing to develop long after most adults have muffled themselves in the cocoon of middle-aged habit and convention." Aldous Huxley

HONORING OUR TRUE SELF

Most people look forward to retirement. A person may have some apprehension for what their future may resemble, yet, few voice their concerns about the impending changes. With the onset of retirement the reality may be different than we expected. Currently, many people are experiencing an earlier retirement because their employers are downsizing. On the other hand, many more people are working into their seventies without any chance of retirement in sight. Many of these employees may have already retired from years of service at a primary employer.

What is unanticipated for some is an impending loss of identity. "I was a head operating room nurse for 30 years. Now the people I see or talk to have no idea of the responsibility I handled all those years." Or, "I retired after 40 years with the same company, and in charge of my division. I'm grateful to be a husband, father and grandfather, but at work I had a sense of value that was different than it is today. As time passes my identity seems more unclear."

It is one thing to retire under anticipated circumstances, and to expect to enjoy the next 20 years. What if there isn't that 20-year-period after retirement? What if a diagnosis comes on the heels of getting that retirement watch? What if all the years as a bread winner, as a valuable employee in your company, and as a resident in your community seem to change over night? Can you sustain your sense of self-worth as your future is altered around you?

Unforeseen circumstances can result in the loss of one's voice, of feeling devalued, unheard, and less respected. As people age they become stereotyped by assumptions for what an aging person can or cannot do, or that their needs are fewer, or less important.

Health care professionals are there with our best interest in mind. Yet, like many professions who are understaffed and over worked, the outcome doesn't always generate a positive experience. Sadly, some stories shared with me by older friends and audience members describe being spoken to in a patronizing way, and treated in a manner which dismissed their emotional well-being. No one likes to feel belittled or disrespected. Ensuring better communication comes down to the way in which we speak or convey our needs to others. This can become a more difficult issue when a patient doesn't have someone to act as a health advocate on their behalf.

What is the responsibility of a health advocate? Caring, being a friend, and being a good listener are desired characteristics of a good health advocate. I've been a health advocate for a single woman whose husband had passed, and who had no close relatives to assist her with her physician or pre-hospital visits. I took thorough notes so we could revisit the doctor's instructions and comments again later. Being a good listener enabled me to provide a sounding board for her decision making down the road—not a decision maker—a listener.

When we are in the seat as a patient, there is often a great deal we do not hear. The doctor is talking, our mind is racing to all the visuals of surgery, to perhaps unwanted and possibly needed treatment, and perhaps even a life cut short of what it was expected to be. Extra ears are beneficial. Emotional support is invaluable.

It is most often expected that a spouse, or immediate family member, would automatically be the best caregiver and health advocate when the need arises. Unfortunately, this is not always the case. When a spouse or best friend is struggling with their own grief, fear, and images of loss, their ability to stand strong and in support of their loved one may be deficient. The fear of suddenly supporting a family on their own without the partner can result in unanticipated behavior.

Immense guilt can burden a mate who is struggling with thoughts of selfishness, all the while aware that the ailing loved one needs support. The grieving companion may stifle their expression of grief and turn outward for comfort. With added guilt about their inability to communicate, or to provide emotional support, they may also resort to withdrawal, or other means of escape. In this situation, it is recommended that both receive counseling to encourage their ability to express themselves. In the beginning, separate counseling might best serve the circumstances. This is why support groups, available to the person who is ill, are so helpful. When able to openly share their feelings among peers of a similar situation, it releases the emotional burden that is harmfully kept inside.

The Shrinking Family Core

It used to be more common for grandparents to reside with their children when they grew older. It wasn't always the case that we routinely found housing for aging parents in nursing homes when they were no longer able to live on their own. In most cultures, the nucleus of the family all resided under one roof, and usually included the grandparents. The grandparents had active roles, when possible, for doing repairs, yard work, gardening, cooking, and helping to care for the children, who were raised respecting the grandparents.

Aging couples are more often able to care for themselves, and to reside for a longer time in their own homes together — especially if one is in better health and able to be the primary caregiver. This is more often the case until one of them passes. When the surviving parent lives in a state away from where their children reside, it may eventually become necessary to move the parent closer for care.

There may be many reasons why the nucleus of the family now less often includes the grandparents; however, the necessity to meet the needs of our aging relative is never less important. While the most considered requirement for care involves residential needs, the emotional and mental needs are sometimes overlooked.

One of the most given responses about aging is fear of becoming a burden to their loved ones. Parents don't always voice what is important to them. When the children have lived away from their parents for years, and especially when the grown children have been focused on raising their own family, their awareness of their parent's preferences, or changing preferences, are seldom known. What sometimes holds a parent back from expressing their desires is that they may have generally put the needs of others before their own, so speaking out now may not be natural to them.

Good Intentions

An example of a well-meaning relative comes from a 90-year-old independent woman who still drives, volunteers, and teaches in her community. Recently, when her relative paid a visit she was left frazzled, saying, "She stopped and got groceries on her way here, but didn't stop to ask what I liked or disliked. She remembered that I mentioned months ago that my garage needed attention; so she cleaned it and emptied the contents as she saw fit. Now I can't find anything, and I'm not sure I was ready to part with some of the things she threw away!"

A phone call from the grocery store to inquire about preferences, allergies, or dislikes would have been one way to demonstrate respect. In 90 years of accumulating what may have looked like clutter to one person, defines another in what may be correspondence, books, collections, heart-held gifts, or travel treasures. Some of the things we accumulate over the years may seem like "stuff," but it is *our* stuff. While we are still a viable, functioning, human being, we want a say in the things which are discarded, and those we are not yet willing to part.

When there is honesty and truthfulness between people, there is a willingness to define what is needed and preferred. Without first reaching this understanding, well-meaning actions and gestures can unwittingly overpower a loved one, resulting in hurt feelings or a sense of threat to their freedom.

When to Proceed with Caution

Not all families function with a core element of integrity. Many families have shared stories about the greed of one or more family members which resulted in bullying, and negatively influencing a parent. Sometimes a family member resorts to verbal abuse, or falsely claiming that the parent is no longer competent of handling their finances. Some resort to threats in order to access the parent's money so they can make the decisions, and spend the parent's money as they see fit. Some go so far as to persuade neighbors, and other family members, of incidents which never occurred to support their allegations. Often there is pressure upon the parent to make changes to their legal will. Sadly, these instances happen more often than one would like to imagine.

When this is the case, it is necessary for the parent to contact an independent and outside source for trust. When money is the issue, it may be necessary to have all arrangements through a reliable attorney outside of the family. When personal safety is involved, speak up. Confide the situation to a trusted friend, peer, or neighbor, and keep them informed. Let them know if things are getting out of hand. Never overlook the need for contacting available resources should law enforcement need to be notified.

Bottom Line

When we have generations treated as if they do not matter, the weave of society unravels under the lack of compassion and respect. Considering a person of any generation who has given and contributed much in their life time as now worthless, or no longer able to contribute, is dishonoring. To revere those who are elders, whose fostering contributed to the strength and infrastructure of the family, is to safeguard the values for future generations.

So whether societal values seem changed, it is in our best interest to value ourselves. It is up to us to designate our finances, to decide what we want our housing and retirement to look like for us—and to not withhold expressing these choices. We look to our society, and our families for a framework that ensures our safety and well being—not unlike what is legally sought for children. We wish to continue our lives with companionship and relationships, community—and especially with dignity. Life at 90 should be no less revered than at any other time in one's life.

1) Can you recall a time when you were treated with less respect than you deserved just because of your age or health condition? Can you think of something that you would do or say differently in that situation if it happened now?

2) Have there been times that you were hesitant or afraid to ask for what you needed from a family member or some sort of caregiver?

3) Do you feel confident in reporting a behavior or language that was inappropriate?

4) Who can you currently trust to confide in if you need assistance or help?

5) Are you currently holding back communicating your needs?

6) What can you identify as your physical, emotional, mental or spiritual needs at this time? Are they being addressed? If not, what can you choose to do or say to encourage they are met?

Chapter Four

"You will know that forgiveness has begun when you recall those who hurt you and feel the power to wish them well." Lewis B. Smedes

LET IT GO

Can you imagine a baby coming into this world with luggage? Probably not; so why do we accumulate it as if we plan to leave with any? If we begin to unpack the baggage we carry of un-forgiveness, so that at any moment in our life it becomes our last, we have released thoughts and emotions which might hinder us at life's end.

There are people who hold tight-fisted to all the unresolved pain of their past. Some people carry their hurt like a travel sticker affixed to the side of a suitcase they carry for the rest of their life. Others display scars from grasping a burning coal intended to throw at another.

Yes, this is all metaphorical for the unresolved issues surrounding forgiveness. How often have we known a friend or family member who may have resided on their death bed still clutching the piece of coal, or with luggage stacked around the room? Perhaps their suffering would have been lessened, or their dying less difficult, had the coal or luggage not existed at all.

Have you ever gone to a high school or family reunion where there arrived a previous adversary? It might have been a cousin who held you underwater nearly too long at the pool. It might be the best friend who ran off with the love of your life behind your back. Maybe the pain stems from an incident that changed the course of your life forever—and you've harbored remorse every day since. The interesting thing is when two such people come together and raise the issue, often only one has held onto the event all these years. Sometimes, the other person doesn't remember, or barely remembers, the incident at all.

Ill feelings, wounded emotions, and immense dislike for this person may have festered beliefs, and caused avoidance over decades. Holding on to the belief, at all cost, may have seemed imperative. It isn't at all uncommon for long held beliefs to end up being a difference of perspective, or a misunderstanding. If we had communicated about it years ago, could we have released it then? Could we have talked it out, gotten it off our chest, and lived our life with more emotional freedom? Could we have lived our life seeing our self and others differently all these years?

It isn't to say that there are not offenses which do break a heart, cause immense loss, physical damage, serious transgressions and even crime. What if we are responsible for a grievous wrongdoing? These, too, seem impossible to excuse.

What if a parent was told lies about a sibling to gain profit, and now the parent has died and the lie remains a haunting of the heart? What if an error cost someone their job, and silence let it happen? What if? For everyone there is a story, and a memory. What can be done about it now? How can we exonerate another, or our self, after all the years, or all the silence?

"If you bring forth that which you have within you, it will save you. If you do not, it will destroy you." Gospel of Thomas

I have worked with people who wished to overcome their memories of victimhood. While I believe there are methods to help release the anger, the pain, and the mental anguish, I know that to call this forgiveness might be false. There is a difference between neutralizing the intense emotions around an incident, and actually experiencing forgiveness. Memories tend to repeatedly call us back to the story— to our identity at that time.

A friend, recalling her mother's situation, explained the following:

"My mom died at age 102. She was raised in a large, and somewhat conservative, religious family. Growing up she had precious few personal possessions. Collecting beautiful things became a priority. These things became more important than the people in her life and their feelings. Her mother died when she was 13. She hadn't been allowed to express her feelings, and wasn't about to begin. The feelings she suppressed were then used unconsciously toward her husband and children in the form of blame, shame, and guilt. She was skilled at shunning others when she didn't approve of what was going on around her.

"Being a hospice nurse, I knew that planning ahead and dealing with unfinished business made the dying process easier for the person dying, and for the family. I attempted, for over a decade, to open a dialogue with my mother—hoping we could solve these issues. Each time I attempted a conversation about her possessions, she would remain silent, then the consequent shunning would last a few days to weeks at a time.

"Two days before her death she asked me for the first time, 'what is going to happen to my things?' I questioned her about what she wanted to do about her many possessions. Her reply was, 'What do you think I should do?' The fatigue and frustration left us with too many decisions and too little time."

Life Is Too Short

It's not difficult to accept the idea that we change every day. We can see that hair shaved yesterday has grown back today. We know that we look different now than five years ago. We change. Our identity changes as well. So many people confuse their identity with other aspects influencing their life. When something has us down in the dumps we loose perspective of other facets of our life. During dark times in our lives things can seem hopeless, like there is no way up, no sunshine coming in, and a muddy picture of our future. We may have a story that is so awful, sad, or unforgettable that it seems justifiable to retain this identity. We will not find happiness in that place, and we have the choice to choose freedom over suffering.

In every moment lies the ability to change for a new, more positive experience. It takes courage to release the old self, yet we are new every moment, and we can create who we want to be. To release something is to be set free. We most often think of the word "liberate" in terms to describe someone being freed from jail, from hostage, or from a restraining country. However, consider what imposed constraints you currently need liberated from in order to have a greater sense of freedom. What real or imagined constraints keep you from being the person you want to be?

It takes courage to release the old self. Some people find satisfaction, or reward, in maintaining and defending that old identity. Some people don't know how not to identify with the victim mentality they may have claimed long ago. They don't know how, or are unwilling, to let themselves experience something vastly different. There is sometimes comfort in the old and familiar habits, like the safety of a routine. Yet many stories, repeatedly told, are memorized to convince ourselves, and others, of our victimhood, our limitations, and our reasons why we can't do, or achieve, or be any way other than we are. These excuses protect us from having to try something different, and from exploring the unknown.

The Buddhists speak of letting go, of releasing that person you were today, and doing so at the end of each day. What they are suggesting is to release any feeling or emotion that made you feel like a victim, and to release any judgment you had about yourself, and anyone else. Surrender any identity that causes you suffering. Let it go. Go to bed, and wake anew.

One way to do this is with a gratitude journal. When we review each day with a grateful heart for all the good we can identify in our life, it helps us to release the negativity. Any negative thought is more apt to become neutralized by thinking about those moments in your day, and for those people in your life, for which you can give thanks.

If you were asked to identify yourself by five descriptive words, what words would you choose? Imagine writing these words on paper, and asked to wear it hung around your neck for a week. These are words of your choosing, so you are more than familiar and comfortable with them. Let's say you display these words for a week, and are asked to reevaluate the words. Do they still most describe who you are? At this time, you may choose to replace one word with a more positive or more uplifting word—if, in fact, it honestly describes you. The following week, if it is fitting, you may again replace one word on your list for a more positive, more accurate word which truthfully portrays you. As you repeatedly evaluate the words you have chosen, your awareness of how you have characterized yourself has increased. Can you now identify with those new words? If you were to contrast your personality and qualities now, to those first five words you chose, would there be more clarity and honesty in the way you recognize and describe your true self?

If we choose to remain in that old identity, might we be the one some day lingering in that bed with the luggage stacked around the room?

Blessing

There is a Taoist principle called *wu wei*. It means *non-doing;* evolving from a place of one's self while relating to others and one's environment. It takes employing a deep understanding to experience, without expectation or judgment, the outcome. It is action, but with release at the very onset—and it is often a way to simply seek peace about *what is*. Let me give you an example.

Many years ago, a friend was hired to paint the inside of our home. He became a friend to my children, and often overheard their concerns. One summer afternoon my youngest daughter was full of angst over a soft ball game to be played later that day. It was just a summer sport, yet not every player saw it that way. The usual pitcher had gone to a girl's soft ball camp. Anyone who didn't take the game as seriously as she did stood to get seriously mocked — and she was generally capable of getting the participation of others on the team to deflate the confidence of one.

This friend listened well to the predicament, looked my daughter in the eye, and said, "Bless her." *What?* He said, "Bless her. That's all you need to do. Don't have any plan. Don't think of other things to say or do. Just show up, and repeat over and over to yourself, 'Bless you.' "

With some reluctance, yet with no other course of action planned, my daughter went to the game. Snide remarks began, yet she kept repeating, "Bless you." The girls got up to bat and did their best, fearing recrimination if their attempt was lacking. Quickly into the game, the intimidating girl began to fall short of her usual flare at the pitcher's mound. After walking eight at bat, she was replaced, leaving the field with her head lower, and no more criticism for her team mates.

"Bless you." Simply two words. No attachment, no judgment, no expectation.

> *"To bless means to wish, unconditionally and from the deepest chamber of your heart, unrestricted good for others."* Pierre Praravand

Compassion

What comes to mind when you think of compassion? Do you think of missionaries working in far off lands feeding and clothing children? Do you think of physicians and surgeons who take time from their work, and travel to another country to perform miracles of caring, and repairing, the lives of others? Do you think of local volunteers who commit to one evening a week to help feed the homeless?

What comes to mind when I ask you to extend compassion to yourself? *Whoa!* Did the screen in your mind just go blank? It takes compassion to forgive another. It takes courage to ask forgiveness. It takes both to forgive ourselves.

Compassion is a melding of higher consciousness with our altruistic being, moving into our heart, creating a peaceful softening, and aligning with a higher resonance. There is no formal protocol, no ten-step affirmation, and no outside coaching. It is a deeply personal and individual pursuit when sought from the most genuine part of our being.

The ultimate power of forgiveness and compassion when attained from this purist possible quest, is that of transcendence which exceeds distance or death. There is nothing which compares, which encompasses the depth of understanding, the release, the healing, and ultimate closure.

I am reminded of the words of Gandhi, "You must be the change you wish to see in the world." If you wish healing outside of you, you must begin within. If you wish to offer genuine compassion to another, it must come first from within yourself.

If I become neutral with the pain from my past,
which imprisoned me within my own thoughts,
I shall release my heavy burden and restriction of my freedom.
I know I shall then move freely from this reality to the next
unfettered, and with peace.

For Further Contemplation

1) Identify an issue, or person connected with this issue, that you can't forgive.

- Challenge yourself to write about what happened, and the way in which this person(s) was involved.

- If you were responsible for what happened, visualize telling each person in each individual incident (take only one incident at a time) that you are sorry.

- Take your time. Visualize making eye contact, and being sincere. Be thorough, as if they were actually sitting across from you.

2) If the wrongdoing was done to you, visualize this person(s) apologizing to you.

- Now, write about what happened (as you did in No. 1) only this time, write a different outcome. Include details, listing everyone involved, what was said or done, and write the story as you wish you could change it.

- Now, taking as much time as is needed, visualize the scenario again, only insert the new ending. Visualize everything as completely as you can. Repeat as often as is needed to change or neutralize your feelings surrounding the original incident.

Should I Choose to Forgive

Old memories crop up in my mind
  (like unwelcome sales people at my door)
  begging my attention to issues hidden in old albums
  and chests in the attic of my brain
Darkness, cobwebs, and time protect and distance me
  from painful recollection
Layers of armor surround my heart
  from days, or years of amassing justification for my pain
A closer glance provokes a wrenching at my heart
  like skin tearing against barbed wire
  in attempt to escape the embrace of the memory
Yet my overburdened heart
  holds a key for every recall I want to banish,
  every face I want to forget, every image that taunts me
Every key unlocks a layer of armor should I choose to...
  should I choose to forgive.

Chapter Five

"There would be nothing to frighten you if you refused to be afraid." Gandhi

FEAR, GRIEF AND COURAGE

In the early 1980s, Dr. Bernie Siegel lectured often around Yale, and other Connecticut locations, before he finished his first book and became the famous oncologist and author he is today. He used to talk for hours, and show slides of pictures that were drawn by his patients which depicted their attitudes about their cancer.

One of the significant things I remember about his talks was his emphasis on people's reactions to their illness. At this point he often became animated, yet very sad, as he spoke of encouraging his patients to make changes in their lives appropriate to the stress, or conditions, which probably contributed to the onset of their cancer.

Sometimes these suggestions would be to get a divorce, to leave a job, to move out of a relationship, or to stand up to a boss or family member. He offered support and understanding to patients who needed to make a choice to improve their health, to allow them a second chance at healing—or survival. The majority of his patient's responses were: *I can't leave my job, Doc. Just cut out the cancer. It would disrupt my family too much to get a divorce, I just can't. I'll take my chances on survival.*

Fear is paralyzing. As we think about the final stage of our lives, what most people fear is loss of control, of mental decline, of becoming a burden to others, of depression, of the dying process, and of pain.

What we believe impacts our reality. Many of our lives are dominated with "what if?" scenarios. *What if I fail the test? What if I don't get the job? What if the tests come back positive?* Our mind doesn't know the difference between actual fact, and a highly emotionally charged "what if?" scenario. When the fear is played out in our imagination over and over again, our body automatically responds to the recurring emotions. Each emotion has a vibration—a resonance. If we entertain that resonance of fear over a period of time, the energy of that frequency draws to us that which we are focusing, or something else that is also on the same vibration.

If initially, we push ourselves to process the scenario further, and follow through with the "what if" thought, then we can conceptualize a possible outcome. This imagined outcome may still be a negative thought. Instead of spending a great deal of time entertaining that idea, ask yourself, *what is the worse thing that can happen?* When we process our fear with this pivotal exercise, our mind shifts into a coping function, and seeks a solution. *What if I fail the test?* I take it over, or do better the next time. *What if I don't get the job?* I look for another one. *What if the tests come back positive?* I listen to the recommendations of the doctor, and chart a course of action. The point is to move out of the rut of thought we most often traverse, and shift mentally toward a resolution. A shift toward the positive won't always guarantee the outcome we want, but the shift from the negative mind set to an up-lifting potential is a step toward hopefulness versus despair.

I'm reminded of the story of the farmer's donkey that fell in the well. The farmer had no way of getting the donkey out, so he began to shovel dirt into the well to bury the donkey. As the soil accumulated, the donkey repeatedly shook off the dirt, and stepped up, until it was high enough to climb out of the well. Our fearful minds sometimes take us to places so deep and dark that we feel there is no way out. This doesn't have to become our reality.

Grief

We most often think of grief as a necessary time to mourn following the death of a loved one. There are other times in our lives, as well, that require grieving if we are to successfully move through a loss. I reference the concept of *moving through* a loss as there are no short cuts, and no way around the elements or stages of grieving.

The grieving one might experience in an abrupt job layoff, a sudden heart attack, or startling diagnosis is well-founded. It is not to say that grief related to any of these examples in any way compares to the grief over the loss of a loved one. It is, however, not uncommon to find that one situation of grieving brings to mind other times when we might have mourned, and didn't. When we don't acknowledge our feelings, or deny ourselves the expression of anger or depression, we inhibit the process that ultimately gets us to the place of understanding, and accepting the loss at the core of our deepest emotions.

The ability to mourn change is relevant to any grieving process. Many people retire and later experience a loss of identity for who they are without their long earned "label of recognition." Imagine a person who has planned, and is about to embark on the vacation of their dreams only to be told that travel is now out of the question due to a looming health condition. We need to give ourselves permission to grieve for freedom lost, and of shattered dreams and goals. Significant changes redefine us. We need to be able to talk out our concerns, our fears, our loss of security, or our identity. Expression is the process by which we are enabled to cope, and empowered to move forward to further process our grief.

Grief is cyclic. Grieving is individual. Not everyone takes the same amount of time to cycle through the progression of grieving, nor do they experience the same stages in order. One may feel the need to rush through their grieving so as to put others at ease, yet, doing so stifles the expression of sorrow that one needs to work through.

It isn't uncommon for people who have been present for us to begin to drop away during the grief processing. Others may grow impatient and just want us return to the way we were. For this reason, it is helpful to be part of a group of people who can identify. People who are experiencing their own grief will not rush, nor belittle another's feelings, but instead will listen and understand.

There are groups, such as counseling groups, hospice groups, church groups and many others, which are formulated for this purpose. Visiting more than one group helps to locate an atmosphere most fitting to your present needs. If it is too soon to participate in a group environment, seek the help of a qualified counselor, or pastoral counselor, who can listen, comfort, and identify suggestions for your progress. You are helping yourself to face your new reality every time you talk about your loss. Talking through your grief helps you to formulate solutions, to find strength, and to move through yet another step to acceptance. I am reminded of an important quote my mother always used to tell me, "This Too Shall Pass."

People who have never suffered a loss may not understand. Refuse to let this stifle your need to express your feelings. Acknowledge the possible need for extra rest. However, if symptoms exceed what you think you can handle, or are recognized as such by a loving and concerned family member or friend, allow yourself the opportunity to discuss your current experience in this process with a qualified professional. No two people ever process an experience in the same way. Respecting ones needs means not being ashamed to seek support and encouragement.

Maintain a schedule. Eat healthy. Get dressed, and get out a little every day. Consider walking, or some form of exercise. Focus on what remains in your life. Find ways daily to be grateful. Write up-lifting sayings on sticky notes, and place them in the bathroom, kitchen, car, and at work to provide cheerful reminders through the day. When possible, give back. Once you find more strength, kindly share your experience and helpful guidance with others who are grieving.

Another way in which people think they are being helpful to someone grieving, is to offer false hope. It seldom seems comfortable to just sit there and listen. Being present with another in their sorrow, their fear, and their adjustment, may be the greatest gift we can offer.

Traumatic Loss

Although resilience is inherent in the usual ability to recover after a significant loss, it takes longer to restore physically, mentally, emotionally, and possibly spiritually, when a traumatic incident, or death, has occurred. Overcoming the shock, disorientation, and sometimes fear, to resume a fully functioning life, can involve a prolonged healing cycle. Symptoms relevant to a traumatic loss are generally more encompassing and pronounced. Evaluation, counseling and therapeutic intervention for recovery may be necessary. Post Traumatic Stress Disorder is at present time a more understood condition, and a variety of therapies are now prevalent to address this syndrome.

Any death for a child involves addressing a wide range of concerns about their present moment, as well as their future. Yet, when children have experienced a traumatic loss, the approach to recovery is slightly different. Like the experience for an adult, the stages are cyclic, and concerns arise in no particular order. However, when a child is overwhelmed, certain behaviors may re-emerge as a way of coping through the confusion. Attempts to adhere to normal and familiar patterns of life, activities, and routines help provide a sense of safety. If children are not supported through the critical time of recovery, the trauma may manifest in intensified fears, nightmares, and heightened emotional and behavioral problems.

Counselors have many tools to assist children in maintaining open communication and necessary expression of their feelings. Play therapies, board games about grief, and certain therapeutic modalities offer a variety of means to work through the trauma and loss. Most schools have some sort of crisis response plan in place to assist upper grade children with their grieving process.

It is important to remember for anyone at any age, what isn't expressed through crying, mourning, and other ways to release the pain, often becomes a symptom, or a behavior when it is retained within.

Courage: Aging Isn't for Wimps

Someone recently said, "I always thought I'd be retired and painting by now. I think I'm working harder now than I did twenty years ago! When do I get to slow down?"

New technology is keeping us alive longer. Early diagnosis, prescription medicine, staying active, and eating with more consciousness for what constitutes healthy food, is all contributing to longevity. Sometimes we get so focused on what prolongs our life, we forget that it still culminates at an end point.

If in our younger years we knew all that we would survive over time, and if we knew all that we would experience in our accumulated years, we would grow old with more reverence for aging.

Every morning, when we pull our feet out of bed and onto the floor, we are preparing to venture from the known to the unknown. From one day to the next, change doesn't seem as ominous. It isn't just when those birthdays roll around that we stop to contemplate our aging. It's looking in the mirror; it's looking at the hands stretching out of our sleeves; it's the first time someone offers you a senior discount; and when it's time to make Medicare choices. When I turned 40, I was unprepared the first time a physician addressed me with the words, "at your age." I estimated that I had another 20 years before that phrase would be addressed to me.

It takes courage to live each day with uncertainty. I recall a bumper sticker that read, "I believe in life *before* death." Sometimes it seems like we are too busy to live our life with the passion and vitality we would like. We tend to give more credence to facts that are measurable. A pulseometer measures your pulse and gives your heart rate. Wouldn't it be interesting if someone created a pulseometer that would periodically let us know that we had sunk into a phase of *barely* living? If we want to make the most of our life, we had better pick ourselves up and move forward toward more fulfillment.

Fortunately, there are rewards in our lives. We are rewarded with the satisfaction of our accomplishments throughout life. No one denies the satisfaction in seeing our children graduate from high school or college, or the joy of holding a new grandchild. We know the rewards of volunteer work, and of helping others. We take pleasure in the accomplishments of friends and family along the way.

I think of the veterans who, when leaving active service, are saluted, patted on the back, and told, "Job well done." I think of corporate employees upon their retirement—the gifts, the parties and the kudos for all their years of commitment. Then what? For many, they enter into an uncertain future about their health, health insurance, finances, housing, and security. Many may seldom ever again be told "Job well done."

We don't think of aging and dying in those terms. When we reach that end-of-life stage, are we met at the end with a smile, a party, pats on the back, and congratulations for a "Job well done?" *Why not*? What can we do to change our current attitude about reaching that finish line? How can we lessen our fear of an uncertain future?

Building a Bridge

Many who have witnessed the dying process agree that one dying without a sense of purpose or completion for one's life is often cited as a foundation for the greatest suffering. When our focus remains negatively on what life has dealt us, we cease to grow beyond the experience. When we are unable to find gratitude for the blessings that were evident, we loose our self to that person trapped in suffering. If our definition of our life is shrouded with the pain we have experienced, we may well reach the finish line clutching dread of only more pain. If we spend so much time and effort looking to the past, how can we move forward with brighter eyes toward any positive anticipation?

When we have set our course, identifying and remaining aware of our purpose throughout our life, we have a stronger sense of courage. When we have clarity about what we believe, and have loved and honored our self and our life, we are more willing to accept that sense of completion, and do so with pride versus regret.

We need to get to a place where we are not living from a mind and heart of fear, but of love. When we learn to love our self unconditionally, loving others unconditionally becomes an extension of the compassion and forgiveness we have accepted for our self. Awaking each day with gratitude is loving *what is*. This is the acceptance. This is the courage. This is the bridge that transforms us from fear and grief. This is the bridge that takes us across the finish line with completion and the confirmation: "Job Well Done."

"We walk by faith and not by sight–not because we are blind, but because faith gives us the courage to face our fears and put those fears in a context that makes them less frightful ... Faith is not a denial of facts; it is a broadening of focus." Rich Mullins

1) Identify a primary fear that you have about your future. Think back to the origins of this thought; does it stem from an early belief system or memory that you better understand today?

2) Can you think of a time that you were unable to grieve sufficiently to experience relief or comfort after a loss?

3) What action now would enable you to complete that unresolved grieving? Would writing about this grief, or sharing this event vocally with a trusted friend, minister, or counselor, help you to resolve it today?

4) List some accomplishments for which you feel pride.

5) Did those around you help you celebrate your "Job Well Done?"

- If not close your eyes right now and visualize the accomplishment.

- Let yourself feel the pride and satisfaction that you felt at the time.

- Now, imagine being surrounded by all of your friends and loved ones.

- Imagine that there is a party to celebrate your accomplishment, and everyone there is stepping up, one at a time, to shake your hand and pat you on the back. As they take your hand, look them in the eye, recognize fully who they are, and let yourself take in their genuine congratulations for a "Job Well Done."

6) Repeat this exercise for each of the accomplishments you have listed.

Chapter Six

"You cannot escape the responsibility of tomorrow by evading it today."
Abraham Lincoln

TAKING CARE OF BUSINESS

Do I have any control over my decisions? Can I change my mind? How can I be sure my wishes will be carried out? Is it possible to die without pain? Why not let others worry about what to do after I'm gone? Have my parents thought of these questions? Are their needs being met? What do I need to know to care for their end-of-life concerns?

One of the fears most frequently expressed by people when speaking about aging, or becoming disabled, is that of burdening their family. Yet, consider the possible burden on the family when no preferences have been expressed. When end-of-life decisions are not made, surviving family members may live the rest of their lives with guilt or grief for not knowing if they made the right choices in the absence of directions by the deceased loved one.

It is in our best interest to have conversations, complete forms, and assign responsibility to trusting family members, or other important individuals in our life, while we are mentally competent and capable of considering our options.

These considerations are essential now, rather than under the duress of pain or recent diagnosis. Better preparation ensures that your wishes will be carried out, that specific details may be honored, whether medically or financially, and that weeks, months, or years can be lived with greater peace of mind about all the detailed preparation completed.

At present time, millions of Americans are uninsured. A lecture presented by a palliative care physician said that the average end-of-life Intensive Care Unit (ICU) stay is approximately nine days, and roughly 38 percent of Americans are placed in an ICU at the end of their life. Thirty-one percent of families use all, or most, of their savings, home or possessions to pay for those nine days in ICU. What do you need to know now to avoid this scenario?

It is important to understand our choices so we can make sound decisions rather than just checking off a box on a form. Family members, when unable to question and communicate to their dying loved one, often wonder if he or she really knew what the verbiage meant next to the box that was checked. It is convenient to have the forms to ponder, yet, it is valuable to speak to people who are knowledgeable, who can clarify the details of the choices, and explain what the possible scenarios might entail.

There are many forms to consider today, and many are available to download from the Internet. Caution should be considered, however, when completing forms. These are legal documents which can be incorrectly drafted, or improperly executed. Accuracy is better assured when skilled people familiar with the documents are consulted, and the appropriate documentation prepared which explicitly expresses the desired wishes. When forms are not well understood, a person can potentially create more problems than they are resolving.

Some questions on Advance Directive documents are explicit regarding the state of being in a coma, or regarding brain damage. There are specific explanations to possible considerations, such as cardiopulmonary resuscitation, mechanical breathing, artificial nutrition and hydration, surgery, chemotherapy, invasive diagnostic tests, and receiving blood, or antibiotics. Additional options that may warrant deliberation include pain medications, and the possible legal prescription of a lethal dose of self-administered medication for a competent, terminally ill adult. A DNR (Do Not Resuscitate) form, if this option is chosen, should be completed, and in some situations, posted where it is easily found, like on the refrigerator door.

Additionally, there are forms to help prioritize your wishes that include: letting nature take its course, being comfortable and pain free, staying mentally alert and competent, and making financial considerations. You need to consider if you wish to remain in your home, or prefer an environment where there are services and community. You need to understand functions and differences between the services of organizations such as Hospice, or Compassion and Choices. You need to keep in mind that the laws vary from state to state.

There may be need for a Durable Power of Attorney to handle the general financial matters. A Durable Power of Attorney for Health Care is similar except this person tends to health care needs and decisions if a client is incapacitated. Usually, this person only makes decisions for you when you cannot. This may be temporary, as in the case of an accident, or long term, if the client is permanently incapacitated.

Why Are These Forms Important to Me?

Your HIPAA Authorization (Health Insurance Portability and Accountability Act) is needed to go along with your Durable Power of Attorney for Health Care, as well as for any family or designated persons you want to have access to your private health care information. You can be denied information pertinent to the health condition of your loved one unless your name is referenced on your family member's HIPAA form. One gentleman in a discussion group attested to being temporarily barred from information about his hospitalized wife because their completed HIPAA forms were on file at the office of their physician, but he did not have a copy of this form on him when she was admitted to the hospital.

The Living Will is a document which applies to the final moments of life, having provided in advance the instructions indicated for artificial life support and organ donation. This form may be called the Declaration as to Medical or Surgical Treatment in some states. A Living Will is not the same as a Last Will and Testament, or a Living Trust.

A Living Will only provides instructions regarding artificial life support measures in the case of an injury, disease, or illness that is not reversible or curable, and is terminal. Often, the Living Will goes into effect when two doctors agree, and put in writing, that you are unable to make your own medical decisions, unconscious, and have a terminal condition. An attorney or physician is not necessary, but may be helpful, to complete a Living Will. In some states, two witnesses who are not health care providers, nor anyone who may inherit property from the injured, ill, or dying patient, must be present.

Other possible considerations include a Medical Proxy for Decision Making, or a Health Care Agent. In some states no one is granted automatic authority in decision making for another adult. Health care providers are only allowed to make decisions for a patient in an emergency, or when the patient cannot make decisions for them selves. These positions are not to be taken lightly. People who are designated need to be aware of your decisions, and know that decisions made on your behalf are expected to reflect your values, goals, and preferences.

There are many resources for Advance Care Planning. Most senior publications list such information, but there are also National Boards for such organizations as Hospice, Compassion and Choices, and other Palliative Care services. Aging with Dignity, the National Alliance for Caregiving, and AARP are also helpful organizations. There are additionally specific support groups for particular illnesses such as Alzheimer's, Parkinson's, AIDS, Cancer, ALS, MS, COPD, Diabetes and others.

Your Planning Is a Gift

Why bother yourself with all of this? Planning and communicating your wishes in advance better assures an end-of-life scenario in which your preferences are honored by all involved. Preparing with attention to detail, and communicating with clarity, is a gift to those you love. Committing to become knowledgeable about these issues and making decisions now, affords you and your family immense peace of mind.

There is nothing worse than conflicting family opinions about what a loved one would want when the person is incapacitated, and the family is under duress at this sensitive time. In spite of all the medical technology capable of extending a life, physicians are not fortune tellers. They can't accurately predict a life expectancy. It is their responsibility to treat the patient unless directions indicate otherwise. When a patient is occasionally lucid they may be asked what course of care they want, but in that state, and during that time, they may not know what it is they want. Additionally, it is often found that your immediate family may not know what your wishes are either. Communication and preparation are your best allies.

Be sure your family, closest friend or designated agent has a copy of your Advance Directives. With the many means of communication today, the person chosen to act as the Medical Proxy for Decision Making, or a Health Care Agent, does not always need to be in the same town. It is essential, however, that the chosen party is a responsible individual who has your best interest at heart. Sometimes your spouse is not the best choice for your health care agent because they may not be emotionally objective. It is important to choose someone who can be trusted to honor and follow through with your specified wishes. Many patients who die in hospital beds made choices which were not carried out; consequently, their final hours were far different from what they, or their families, wanted. Survivors need to know of your decisions, and discussions should take place so they are not surprised later and demand to contest your choices.

How to Bring Up the Conversation

When a family member refuses to discuss any end-of-life decisions, great tact is required to gently bring up the topic in an acceptable way. Without resorting to aggressiveness, questions that address their worries about their future may be raised. Initiating a conversation about a relative or friend who experienced a traumatic incident for their loved one, because no directives had been established, may get everyone to participate in the discussion. If the conversation doesn't get very far the first time, try again another time. Reminiscing about family members who have passed is another way to enter into a pertinent conversation. Also, diligent note-taking is important so information shared is not forgotten or overlooked. (Note: Please refer to the "Role Play Demonstration Script" in Appendix A-2.)

Today there are many forms of media to help bring up the topic. There are many movies and TV shows which deal with hardships, and end-of-life decision making. There are discussion groups, and panel presentations presented at churches, and social organizations who wish to promote and emphasize that this decision making process, and the completion of these forms, are just as important as having a will.

With the baby-boomer generation nearing this higher age status we might refer to the necessary process of communicating our final wishes as *the talk*. Notoriety was generally given to this generation for the spawning of so much open talk about sex. Now mid-lifers would rather educate their children about sex than engage in an end-of-life talk with their parents.

There is relief by having at least one of the two parties break the ice. Sometimes the parents hold back from these conversations. Other times, the parents want to talk and the children are the ones covering their ears in denial. It is more appropriate for the parents to initiate the conversation. Siblings may question the motives of other siblings who bring up the topic if the parents are not the ones commencing the dialogue. Begin exploring the topic with conversations about beliefs and values. Address spiritual thoughts, and what personal guidance you'd like most to pass on to your children and grandchildren.

Wouldn't our final days prove more meaningful for us if we made our wishes known and initiated our preparations ahead of time? The satisfaction of having choices in place, assignments made to trusting agents, and the understanding of the final wishes expressed, better assures peace of mind for all involved.

For Further Contemplation

1) If time allows, begin with an outline to initially address the topics in categories; separate those topics of emotional and spiritual content from those which require conversations with a lawyer, assigning responsibilities to a chosen agent, or involving witnesses and further documentation.

2) Diligent note-taking is helpful so pieces of information shared are not forgotten or overlooked.

Chapter Seven

"If you ask me what I came to do in this world, I will answer you: 'I am here to live out loud'" Emile Zola

WHAT AM I WAITING FOR ?

If there is someone you need to tell "I'm sorry," tell them today. If there is someone you need to remind that you love them, what are you waiting for? We are always putting things off. Why wait until tomorrow for something which gives such pleasure today? If there is something we have always wanted to do, why are we waiting for permission? From whom are we waiting permission?

What have you put off? A change for the better always starts with one step. We need to accept that we have possibilities. We don't have to live the rest of our lives convincing ourselves, and others, that change is impossible. We can choose to make a difference if we want our lives to look different.

People frequently speak of how exhausted they are. It makes us exhausted when we are not being true to ourselves. We maintain a constant busyness, yet, sometimes we need to just say no. Continued, and excessive, stress frequently leads down a road to illness. In an attempt to cope with too much stress, many consider a course of escape. How many times have you wanted to pack your bags and run away from a demanding life? Few get to do that. Yet, many spend their life escaping on a regular basis—with alcohol, prescription or recreational drugs, smoking, sleep, and food. Sometimes people become workaholics to escape other demands in their lives.

When we treat ourselves with the respect that we deserve, and make choices that demonstrate that respect, we have more energy for the life we want to live. When we allow ourselves the choices that make us happy, we are energized.

We can become experts at convincing ourselves that we are happy the way things are. When was the last time you asked yourself—am I happy? How would you answer that today? How many of us say something like, "Well, I'd be happier *if*...." Or, "I'll be happy *when*...." Do we become happy by leaving it to chance? We believe we'll be happy down the road when something occurs which allows us to become happier then, than now. What we believe impacts our reality.

> *"The tragedy of life is what dies inside a man while he lives."*
> Albert Schweitzer

Choice, Not Chance

As a patient with a disease that affected the connective tissue of his body, and with no known treatment cure, Dr. Norman Cousins wrote *Anatomy of An Illness*. He improved the quality of what time he had left to live because of his self-empowerment and positive attitude. He emphasized that belief in recovery is so important, and that all the medical intervention should not over shadow the role of the patient.

We know, too, that when we are surrounded with a negative and judgmental environment, our beliefs can be undermined, and the success of our healing process can become compromised. A client of mine called when her mother was diagnosed with breast cancer. She had pleaded with her mother to consider alternative methods to chemotherapy to address the cancer. When I asked what her mother wanted to do, the client gave a doctor's name, and explained the surgery, chemotherapy and radiation the doctor recommended. This wasn't the choice the daughter wanted for her mother, nor was she very happy with my response. I urged my client to refrain from telling her mother that her choices were wrong. If her mother is convinced of this path, and has faith in this physician and in his recommendations, then supporting and encouraging the mother through her healing process may be the loving and caring action she needs to survive.

When I moved across the country years ago, a friend gave me a sign that read, *Choice—Not Chance—Determines Destiny*. This is still relevant today.

Living by choice IS living consciously. Sometimes we deny that we do have choices. We go through our days like robots on a tight time schedule announcing "I have to do this… I have to go there… I have to be at this meeting…." We not only perform this ritual ourselves, but enlist our entire families in the parade of *must do's*.

One client of mine always complained of back pain. Sometimes she couldn't even stand straight. Almost every visit she said, "I just can't get him off my back," and continued to carry on this conversation about her husband. Every week when she left she felt better, yet, upon arrival at each subsequent appointment she was again in the same condition. We discussed the impact of her emotions to her physical state, yet options, especially divorce, were out of the question. She had subscribed to the role of victim, of increased unhappiness, and an eventual serious diagnosis. Ask yourself—am I living the life I want to be living? If not, what would that look like?

A general surgeon who understood this connection between the body and emotions, and with years of surgical experience, once sadly expressed that by removing certain organs or tissues, he had eliminated the body's voice that was attempting to communicate the presence of some deeper emotional or spiritual concern which had been ignored, and needed attention.

> *"The sorrow which has no vent in tears may make other organs weep."*
> Henry Maudsley

Must it take a life or death issue, such as a threat of terminal cancer or some other major disease process, to change our ingrained habits and beliefs? We need to stop and evaluate our choices.

Waiting for Permission?

Are we waiting for someone to give us permission to make changes in our life? Are we not willing to give ourselves permission to choose ways to live healthier, with more peace and more joy?

Over the years technology, and pharmacology, have seemingly become more important than the role of our doctor. The hallmark of a family doctor was someone who knew, and really listened to the patient. Time constraints, and today's emphasis on various testing, may preclude taking into consideration lesser factors which may lie at the root of the symptoms.

A young client had been to many doctors for a diagnosis and for answers to her symptoms. No one could find anything essentially wrong with her. Due to her illness, she left her corporate job and devoted her days doing odd jobs to get by, and attending to various doctor visits. She was currently very happy, but maintained her litany of ills. I gently confronted her one day with the question, "If you were well what would that mean for you?" Her eyes dropped in silence, and then she answered, "I'd have to go back to my corporate job. My parents and friends would expect me to work at a job like I had before—a job I didn't like—and for the amount of money they'd expect me to again earn."

Must we experience a diagnosis or illness to begin to listen to our heart, or follow our dreams? Ask yourself—who am I waiting to give me permission to live my life? What would I rather my life look like? Am I living a meaningful life?

Maybe a drastic change is required. Yet, maybe beginning with one or two small changes will help to prioritize values, dreams, and goals. Honestly, consider these questions: what have I have always wanted to do, or to become, that I have put off? Could I be happier? Could I be more at peace? Is there a change that would help me take better care of myself mentally, physically, spiritually, and emotionally?

Every Day–A Special Occasion

Years ago the following story appeared in the *Los Angeles Times* by Ann Wells:

> "My brother-in-law opened the bottom drawer of my sister's bureau and lifted out a tissue wrapped package.
>
> "'This,' he said, 'is not a slip. This is lingerie.' He discarded the tissue and handed me the slip. It was exquisite; silk, handmade and trimmed with a cobweb of lace. The price tag with an astronomical figure was still attached. 'Jan bought this the first time we went

to New York at least eight or nine years ago. She never wore it. She was saving it for a special occasion. Well, I guess this is the occasion.' He took the slip from me and put it on the bed with the other clothes we were taking to the mortician. His hands lingered on the soft material for a moment, then he slammed the drawer shut and said, 'Don't ever save anything for a special occasion. Every day you're alive is a special occasion.'"

It takes courage to view ourselves from a perspective other than the way we have grown accustom, and to make the changes that might offer us a better quality of life. Every day you're alive is a special occasion.

After including Ann Wells' quote in a message I delivered at a speaking engagement, an elderly lady pushing her husband in a wheel chair approached me. She was excited to tell me that she was moved by what I had said, and was going to go right home and get out her good china. She said, "Why am I waiting for a special occasion to use it? I'm going to begin enjoying it more right now!" The lady behind her chimed in with her revelation as well, saying, "I've been putting off writing my memoirs. I thought people would think it was silly, but I'm going to get started on it right away."

One of my favorite lines from the movie, *Serendipity*, is as follows:

"The Greeks didn't write obituaries. They ask only one question after a man died. 'Did he have passion?'"

Empower yourself with the fact that you do have options. Let yourself become motivated to finish what you are here to do. Whether you are 25 or 105, make a commitment to live every day with passion. Learn to recognize the beauty in living gratefully and consciously every day.

"Death isn't a spooky thing. Death teaches us the value of time.
We realize how precious it is. We realize we don't have forever!"
Leo Buscaglia

1) Am I investing my time in the people and things that matter most to me?

2) Do I set aside quality time for myself?

3) Am I living the life I want to be living?
      Am I living a meaningful life?
      Am I living a purposeful life?

4) Who am I waiting to give me permission to live my life more fully?

5) Could I be more at peace? What would give me more peace of heart and mind?

6) Is there a change that would help me take better care of myself mentally, physically, spiritually and emotionally?

A Lit Candle

Step up now to reclaim your life
  and receive your understanding
  that will sustain you in the days to come.
Don't look back to worry about
  what you may leave behind.
What lies before you offers you more peace, more calm,
  than you can know in your experience
  in this life thus far.

You cannot erase your knowing.
There is no going back to the darkness
  once the candle has been lit,
  no return to hovering in fear in the dark
  once the space of consciousness has been illuminated.

Chapter Eight

"Some people think they are in community, but they are only in proximity. True community requires commitment and openness. It is a willingness to extend yourself to encounter and know the other." David Spangler

COMMUNITY AND REMEMBRANCES

Growing up in a small rural community, I didn't appreciate everyone knowing each other's "business." It seemed to me that one need only to confide a bit of news, or a problem to the local hair dresser or barber on Friday, and by Sunday morning the whispering had commenced from one pew to the next in church.

Years later, however, my observation of this networking changed. Everyone knew my dad. Born and raised in the area, his life was honored when he returned home from World War II, and again with the gun salute at his funeral. After my mother passed away, my father usually frequented one of two restaurants in a nearby town for his meals. If he ever missed a meal when he was expected, a phone call went out to a neighbor to check on his whereabouts. That accountability for an aging, single man in his community is envious.

There are many such groups of men and women who meet on a regular basis for breakfast, or some agreed upon meal, for support and camaraderie. Small communities of people meet who exhibit common interest and common concern for each other. This might resemble a knitting group, a bridge club, a gathering of mothers during a children's playtime, or regular customers meeting after work in a bar. In my dad's case, when not farming or fixing equipment, some of the guys hung out at the garage in town. I can recall the familiarity of this as if I were looking at a Norman Rockwell painting. This is community. These people care about each other, feed each other, celebrate each other's good news, commiserate the bad, and are there for each other to the end.

I recall when a farmer may have been injured, or ailing, during the planting or harvesting season. As soon as the other farmers had finished their own land, they headed to the farm of the downed farmer, finishing his planting or harvesting that needed to get done, even if it meant working into the night or in shifts around the clock. Today, some people hardly know their neighbors well enough to take part in neighborly gestures, but once a kind deed is initiated, the habit of caring reciprocation begins. Whether it is shoveling the sidewalk for an elderly person living next door, preparing food for a neighbor who just returned home from surgery, or being on standby to care for an older sibling when the parents rush to the hospital in labor with a new baby, it is inherent within us to want to be of assistance.

Families are spread out across the country, and sometimes across the world. Our many recent generations have become ever more transient. Yet the need to be included, and the need to love, and to be loved, is never lost. Community is essential to our well-being. From time to time magazine articles speak to the importance of community, and its impact on one's health. Some suggest that those who live in isolation are more apt to experience heart disease. Individuals who may be predisposed to depression, because they are alone or grieving, often feel better when they get out and participate in group activities or social events. When people have others in their life that they look to as a support group, of people they can confide in or have things in common with, they are also found to have stronger immune systems. We have a responsibility to be part of that community for others.

"The process of really being with other people in a safe, supportive situation can actually change who we think we are... And as we grow closer to the essence of who we are, we tend to take more responsibility for our neighbors and our planet." Bill Kauth

Being Fully Present to Another

In the 15th Century in Christian literature there is record of oral teaching and small booklets issued for the purpose of assisting friends and family in the preparation of their loved one which would lead to "a good death" and salvation. Many people couldn't read, but the pocket pamphlets in Europe contained pictures depicting the preparation process:

- instructing the dying of what to expect,
- assisting with final preparations for their possessions,
- encouraging actions and attitudes toward repentance,
- forgiving others and asking for forgiveness,
- witnessing their address to God their readiness,
- seeking God's guidance,
- offering prescribed prayers requesting help and protection,
- and awaiting the arrival of an angel to come and receive the soul of the deceased.

A 21st Century interpretation is no less important today:

- Acknowledge the suffering through the process of denial, and subsequent stages, to acceptance of the reality of death.
- Offer genuine support without shirking the responsibility of what needs done.
- Assist with getting affairs in order.
- Help with the understanding of decisions which need to be addressed.
- Console, offer reassurance, and remain honest in communication.
- Offer no false hope.
- Provide genuine demonstration of compassion, care, and touch.
- Ensure the presence of medication to give relief of pain and symptoms.
- Offer prayers,
- and ensure needs are addressed physically, mentally, emotionally and spiritually.

"Provision for others is a fundamental responsibility of human life."
Woodrow T. Wilson

Before becoming a toddler, one strives to walk without assistance. Teens and young adults exert a growing self-reliance in their goal for autonomy and individualism. It is our nature to pursue a life of self expression, of few restrictions, and of freedom. What is not in our nature is the relinquishing of those achievements.

Surrendering to the aid of others for intimate care requires trust. Being present to a loved one during illness, or vulnerability, is sacred. Gently discussing the ways you can help, and gradually taking on more tasks as needed, encourages one's ability to accept and receive. Demonstrating a willingness to completely care for a loved one helps them to release their need for independence.

As people view possibilities for the end of their life, fears often expressed are the threat of abandonment, isolation, of dying alone, suffering and pain, deception by those around them—those caring for them, and regrets over wasted years or opportunities.

To participate at this intimate time requires being present, able to listen without judgment, and without forcing the process to meet any time constraints. Being deeply compassionate, and listening with heartfelt understanding, assists in working through denial, anger, depression, bargaining, and final acceptance. Preparation in this way contributes to a sense of hope, reassurance, and ultimate completion.

Remember Me

My daughters have already heard some of my favorite stories a few times. I guess that's the beauty of either telling your story to someone new who hasn't heard it before, or telling your story to someone you are sure will forget, so they won't mind hearing it again. Either way, we are blessed to have the stories that we cherish. We are fortunate to have the experiences to draw upon that we enjoy recalling again and again.

It has been said that focusing on a pleasant memory, one that embraces genuine happiness, and which generates a positive feeling, is good for the body. This combination is thought to heighten the resonance by which we draw more happiness and well-being to ourselves. Isn't it a pleasure to be around people who are happy and love sharing their experiences? Isn't it great when we can identify with their antics, some similar history, or hearing a memory of another that reminds us of when we did such and such? It is delightful to recall good times. Of course, we've all had our losses, our dark night of the soul, or our hard-knocks. Yet, it is the good times that we want to acknowledge to outweigh the challenging times.

Sometimes we are discouraged from recalling these tales to people who have heard them before. Commencing to share a favorite memory is sometimes met with mocking or abrupt interruption, "Yea, we've heard that one!" Stifling this expression is like suppressing one's happiness. Who should be cheated out of a dose of happiness? One day, the telling of these stories will be missed—and who tells them better than the person from whom the memory originated.

Sometimes stories reveal lesser known information about our friend or loved one. It is in the stories that we sometimes get a glimpse of something we never knew before, and an understanding for a particular behavior, or reluctance to discuss a specific topic.

My daughter was given an assignment in elementary school to ask questions of an elderly relative about their life, and write about it. The answers my father gave her surprised me. Being raised a Quaker who served in World War II, he always refrained from answering questions asked of him about the war. Some of the comments he made to my daughter, however, revealed priceless gems of information about my father's life he had never before discussed.

Our stories are about milestones, of where we have been, with whom we have shared our life, of those whose influences shaped us, and of those whose lives we left our imprint as well. Our stories are like a treasure map, unbeknownst to us at the start, of the treasures we would find along the way—nevertheless, a squiggly map of our life coursed over the years.

These stories of our journey need to be recorded for posterity. They are historical tidbits that bear witness to our existence. They reveal character, values, a life well lived, and a life well loved.

Our stories—these reflections about our lives—reveal who we were, and who we have become. They are colorful pieces of our lives, and as the pieces of who we are come together, the final puzzle piece, our final story is on hold, to be pressed into place at our closing.

1) Who is your "community?"

2) Do you have a sense of belonging? If not, what do you think you can do to become more involved in a group of people whose company you would value?

3) Have you recorded any of your favorite stories?

4) What memories stand out that you want remembered by your loved ones?

Eventual Wisdom

We live our life as if it will go on indefinitely,
taking risks, challenging our Creator
as if we can't be caught
because we think ourselves immortal.
As we get older we generally reel in that brash attitude
and exchange it for bartering.
Later, we expect in some way the inevitable
and wait to see what we are dealt
weighing the reality as it unfolds.
Taking each day slower, taking in more sunsets, and
being grateful for each new sunrise,
we embrace the remaining in-between time.

Chapter Nine

"As you write your last chapter, know that this day shall mark the birth of your greatest awareness. Focus not on fear, nor sadness. Reach up to the grace that awaits to carry you forward to beauty you have not imagined." Judith Haynes

TRANSFORMATION

Author, J. Phillip Jones, in his book, *Light on Death: The Spiritual Art of Dying* says, "We have looked at the stages of grief due to losses associated with the death of a loved one. But what has not been lost? What can never be taken away from us? There are three important things about our loved one's life that remains with us:

> The memory of our loved one
> The legacy of our loved one
> The love we still share"

We want to acknowledge that we were here, with a purpose, and that our life mattered. We want to be remembered for who we were, and what we did with our life. We are all here as witnesses for each other, to validate others, and to be validated. We want to leave memories of having loved.

We want to live on through the memories of our loved ones. We want the legacy of our love, our values, and our ideals to resonate down through the lives we leave behind, to leave hearts touched in ways that are passed on—and remembered.

What dies? The body, the shell that housed our soul, withers. Yet no demise can lessen the love which remains throughout all time in our hearts.

Our lives are indeed journeys. This journey, as we know it, may end. It may continue in a way that goes on without the limitation of the body as its vehicle. Life is not about the ending; it is about the living. It is about living well. It is about our interaction with our world, and our relationships with all whom we come into contact during this journey. It is about the emotions felt, the risks taken, and the lessons learned.

We recall our experiences, and our relationships, as we process our lives. The essences of our relationships remain with us, a part of us, as we remain a part of them. Neither time, nor space, separates the residing energy of that love when one dies.

We prepare to renew. We grasp the full recognition of our essential self. We enter into the consciousness of leaving behind the duality, which has become increasingly discernable over time.

To die is not the ending. It is a unification of our core self with our world, our Universe, and all that is again without limit.

When I ended the eulogy I wrote and read at my mother's funeral, I said the following:

> "There is so much that we don't know, nor understand about death. But through our faith, we believe that the future existence is a release unto God's presence—the Source of all—giving back to God that which He created. God's blessing to her parents was her birth. His blessing to us was her living, and His grace for us is in our remembrance of her. Let us give praise and thanksgiving for her life, for having known her as a wife, a mother, a grandmother, a great-grandmother, a sister, an aunt, a cousin and a friend. Let us give thanksgiving for her living, and rejoice now in her release from suffering and pain. We can never forget that she died. But we will always remember that she lived."

Stretch Your Imagination

Our images of dying were born to us out of fear, and usually of witnessing the passing of friends and loved ones. Were it not for those images, what images might we conjure up on our own? From our imagination and desire for what we wish the after life to be, what can we hold in our minds instead of that which we have visualized all our lives? Can we paint in our mind an image that is serene, peaceful, and filled with love and awe? Can we entertain ideas out of the ordinary for what our future "over there" might consist of?

Many have already conceptualized the potential for simply "walking through the veil" of difference between this world, and another existence. Sometimes, I use an image like the walk way that bridges the airport to a plane, or of a boat docked at the end of a long pier—waiting to transport me across the calm lake to the other side. Other times, I visualize a handful of family and friends waiting for me at the beginning of a brilliantly lit tunnel. A representation of a portal which allows you, by choice, to enter and willingly be bridged to all that is waiting on the other side, is a useful image to envision.

What If We Dare to Imagine That We Might Choose Our Time?

My grandfather lived to his mid 90s. He was hospitalized after a fall that broke his hip. When he was told that he would soon be transferred to a nursing home for recuperation, his spirit was broken, too. He couldn't be cared for at home during recovery, as his wife of over 70 years, and also in her 90s, was a tiny woman compared to his 6-foot frame. He died within hours—not living long enough to be transferred to the nursing home.

My father died at 82. He was relatively healthy. A neighbor of his addressed me at a viewing the day before his funeral. He told me that my dad had driven to his house the week before, and admitted having trouble with his vision. I'm sure my father did not reveal this information to family for fear of a pending discussion that would most likely result in forfeiting his car keys. My father depended upon his car to get him to breakfast and lunch each day—a time he loved to socialize with his peers and other locals, as much as to partake of a good meal. To surrender the keys to his car was too much sacrifice for this proud man. He died within the week of a heart attack that took him quickly.

Can we be so bold as to imagine that we might take up this new journey without pain in our transition? We know medication is available to us at life's end to ease vacating the physical body. Can the preparation we begin today, subscribing to greater awareness, forgiving, and making amends, allow us to come to our end without suffering? Is it possible, as our awareness expands, we might manifest that which we have painted in our minds for a fearless, pain-free, journey home?

Many, by increasing numbers, and documented in books and research, are well aware of the souls on the other side wishing to communicate to those here and now, that they are waiting. Their communication is often to a survivor immediately after their own passing, and with the intention to convey that they are safe, and that dying should not be feared.

An acquaintance shared a current stress in her life. She was deciding upon whether or not to place her mother in a nursing home. Her reason for considering this was because her mother was suddenly having conversations around the house with family members who had already died. Although her mother was very ambulatory, and fairly self-sufficient, this recent course of events had the woman baffled. I suggested perhaps her mother was nearing her transition, and was communicating with those on the other side who were there to comfort her, dismiss her fears, and ease the process.

The first hospice patient that I was assigned, spoke of her family members who had died — her husband, a son, and two brothers. As we got to know each other, she shared her stories with me. Her level of trust allowed her to be open with me in her conversations about these people. Some days later, as she talked about one or the other, her eyes drifted off, and her conversation paused as if distracted by a vision only she could see. As she neared her last day, this happened more frequently, until she was nearly always in this "in-between" place.

Farewell

At some point in this journey — this beautiful releasing experience — it is okay to let your family know that you are making peace with all that is happening — and ask your family, your friends, and your loved ones that they lovingly let you go when the time comes.

Hearing is the last sense to go, and that fact should be made known and reiterated to all who care for the elderly, the dying, and all family who enter or speak in the dying person's room. Too commonly, people assume that if the patient looks asleep, they are beyond detection of what is being said. Even though the patient may seem asleep, or beyond the ability to communicate, it is meaningful to share stories, to play soothing music, and to speak of good memories.

Enveloped with love, and drifting asleep to the tender words of a loved one, is an experience we have cherished since our childhood. The caring experience and loving expression is no less important now than embraces of celebration we received when we entered this world.

Some Call It Heaven—I Call It Home

As in all that is cyclic, we disconnect in order to re-connect. We do so to be born, and we do so again as we leave this physical body. Reuniting, redefining with the core of who we are, we come to know ourselves again—not as we are now on the *outside*—but at the essence of our true self within.

We are here to live in the present—choosing to stand apart from energies which are not in harmony to our higher self—yet never separated from the Source of our being. We are not here to waste time on negativity. We are here to cultivate the regularity of gratitude and forgiveness for our self, and for others. We are here to live for the greater good. We are here to develop our soul, to grow and expand our consciousness toward Spirit, to evolve, and to transcend this reality.

Let the final chapter of your life be an expression of participation equal to that which you have demonstrated in living. Allow yourself the accomplishment of empowerment upon your farewell. Let this be your legacy to those remaining, that their perception of the end-of- life may be changed by bearing witness to this wisdom. This transition need not reside in darkness and fear. Instead embrace this time to come together in love and open sharing.

We come to a place of understanding—greater than ourselves—that is aware of this re-aligning with our true core, our authentic self. This is a melding of not only who we are now, but that which we have always been—for our soul knows neither separation, nor age.

"Nothing is hidden that will not become evident;
nothing is secret that will not be known and come to light." Luke 8:17

For Further Contemplation

1) Think of someone whose legacy has been a gift to you throughout your life.

What do you want your legacy to be for your loved ones and friends?

2) Take time to sit quietly.

Allow yourself to paint in your mind an image that is serene, peaceful, and filled with love and awe?

3) Now see yourself in that image of what your afterlife might look like.

Hold this thought in your focus. Let the peacefulness envelope you, and give you peace of heart and mind.

"Nothing is worth more than this day." Goethe

Affirm the following declaration:

Each day I give thanks.

Each day I pronounce with gratitude:

THIS IS THE FIRST DAY OF THE REST OF MY LIFE!

TODAY my priority to *fully* live this day is to

_____

_____

_____

TODAY...
my focus is on *now*, this moment,
the fullness of this very moment.

TODAY...
I give myself permission to live this day as I choose.

I give myself permission to complete this day in a way
that makes me happy, and in a way in which I feel
empowered about my life.

And The Truth Shall Set You Free
by Judith Haynes

It validates not the truth of who you are
to contemplate failure
upon leaving this place on this planet.

Why must we think that our testimonial
to those left behind is that we failed
because we are mortal?

Why must we think more about disappointing the doctors
or disappointing our families
than to ask for celebration and encouragement
for our journey forward?

Why cannot we ask of those who love us ...
of those who have cared for us, of those kindred to our hearts
who have indeed witnessed our presence, witnessed our deeds
witnessed our journey
to again witness with us
our gratitude for this dance, this time of play or drama
on this earth
this time scripted in this role, with this cast among us
*to celebrate, to celebrate—**to celebrate***
—and to release us
cheering us on to our next journey
our next dance
our next role
and cast of characters
wherever that may be.

Group Discussion Questions

The following format is very helpful for families, church groups, counseling groups and anyone wishing to initiate deeper conversation with others about the content of this book. It is highly recommended that group participants also obtain a copy of the succeeding book in this series, *My Life Well Lived: A Journal of My Journey*. The completion of that book can commence while reflecting on all the issues reviewed in this text. Openly discussing the following questions in a group environment is greatly beneficial in encouraging the acceptance of the topic, and opening to one's most intimate thoughts and beliefs. These discussions prime the participant to best, and most honestly, respond to the questions in the journal.

Chapter 1... A Conscious Journey

1. As a group, discuss the words that first come to mind when thinking about death or dying?

2. Discuss why most people are in denial about dying? Why is it such a taboo topic?

3. Individually recall your first experience with a death or a funeral.
   • How old were you?
   • How did it make you feel?
   • Try to remember the details from that experience that shaped your current beliefs about dying.
   • Write some notes on what you remember, then discuss these questions in groups of two or three.

4. Address the following questions individually, and then open for a group discussion:
   • Recall a specific family or religious belief system about dying that you were raised with or influenced you.

- During your life, what other belief systems about dying (such as other religions or cultural beliefs) have you become aware of, and what, if anything, have you since integrated into your thinking from that added knowledge?
- To this day, what has been your most significant experience about death or dying?

Allow some time within the full group setting to discuss specific questions or concerns pertaining to this chapter.

Chapter 2... No Time for Silence

1. In groups of two, discuss the earliest dialogue you remember with family, relatives, someone at church, a teacher or a friend about death.

- Who was it with?
- When was this?
- What was the discussion as you recall it?
- Did the dialogue happen because of the death of a pet, relative or friend?
- What, if any, impression did this leave on you?
- Come back to the group and share some of the comments.

2. When one is able to communicate genuinely and honestly to family members, friends, physicians and caregivers, it is a blessing and relief to all involved. To be able to express emotions, concerns and decisions openly is not only empowering, but freeing.

Sometimes it takes a lot of nerve to want to share thoughts, feelings and wishes with others for fear of condemnation and judgment. It may be difficult to find the courage to confide in someone about a concern that is worrisome for fear of their response.

As a group, take each of the following responses separately and discuss your reaction and feelings when someone you are speaking with replies with:

"Oh, that's silly."
"Don't worry."

"Oh, I know exactly how you feel."
"Oh, you shouldn't think that way."
"You're going to be fine."
"You can beat this thing, just hang in there."

3. Individually, address yourself with the following statement, "Perhaps it is others who are trying to communicate with me and are being met with my resistance to engage in an open discussion."

In groups of two, contemplate the following questions and honestly answer these questions:

- How can I improve upon my communication skills?

- Who do I need to have a conversation with now, and what is it that needs said?

- What changes in my expression or tone of voice makes others uncomfortable in their attempt to discuss important issues with me?

- What can I do to encourage an open discussion?

4. Reviewing the advice in Chapter 2, discuss with the group what you learned that you might now adapt to improve your communication skills?

5. Divide the group into groups of two. Take the one skill you identified in Question 3 that you want to improve upon; then, create an imagined conversation using this new approach to better communicate. Remember to maintain eye contact, and allow yourself this opportunity to select the topic that is close to your heart for this exercise. Then take turns practicing skills you wish to improve.

Allow some time within the full group setting to discuss specific questions or concerns pertaining to this chapter.

Chapter 3... Honoring Our True Self

1. As a group warm-up, go through the list below and suggest definitions for each item listed. After a period of time, form groups of two or three people and discuss these categories, and how they relate personally.

Physical Needs	Emotional Needs
Mental Needs	Spiritual Needs
Community	Social Needs
Safety	Dignity
Companionship	Health Advocate

Identify and note your comments. Considering your own network of family and friends, contemplate the words relative to these relationships.

2. Note if your needs are being met within each of these categories, or if there is something lacking that needs attention.

Allow some time within the full group setting to discuss specific questions or concerns pertaining to this chapter.

Chapter Four... Let It Go

1. As a group, discuss:

- What are the first things which come to mind when asked, "What baggage are you carrying around every day?" Examples: Money spent unwisely; something said or done to hurt another; beating yourself up over lack of success or poor decision making.

- Imagine pictures of suitcases. Draw rectangles on a sheet of paper to represent this luggage. What label(s) would you affix to each bag? Allow time for everyone to address their own answers and make notes about the emotions, the issues of forgiveness or other remembrances they carry with them year after year.

- Now draw circles the size of your fist on a page. Within these circles write the name(s) of people you have clutched a burning coal during your life, with the intention to cast at another. Example: Someone I haven't forgiven for the way they spoke to me, treated me, or embarrassed me.

2. Allow time for group members to individually address the following question:

If I could die with a clear conscience and knew that doing so depended upon forgiving the following people, here is a list of those people, and what I need to forgive them for:

3. Sometimes there are smaller offenses that come to mind, but generally there may be only one person for whom betrayal or serious resentment has prevailed over the years. Discuss as a group the ways in which people have successfully experienced forgiveness. Open discussion on forgiveness may help those in the group who are currently struggling with forgiveness issues.

4. Discuss as a group whether or not it is harder to forgive another, or harder to forgive one's self. Individually address the next question:

- The most important person I may not have forgiven in my life is ME. Because of the way I, or someone else, held me accountable for this, I have never been able to forgive myself for:

- Go home and journal about this question this week.

- Write a letter to yourself, acknowledging the issue you have identified, and lovingly write statements of forgiveness to yourself. Use your own name in the beginning salutation, as well as throughout the letter. Sign your letter with your name, followed by the words, *Your Higher Self.*

- Now read the letter to your self out loud.

- Repeat the reading of this letter out loud daily until the issue has become less significant to you emotionally, and you feel genuine forgiveness for yourself.

Allow some time within the full group setting to discuss specific questions or concerns pertaining to this chapter.

Chapter 5... Fear, Grief and Courage

1. As a group, discuss the reasons why fear seems synonymous with the thought of dying.

2. Go around the group and specifically name many of the primary fears surrounding the thought of dying. Example: Two mentioned

in the chapter are loss of control and becoming a burden to others.

- Have someone write on a board or take notes on the answers given in the group.
- Take each answer, one at a time, and more deeply examine the fear. As uncomfortable as it may be, identifying and discussing the fear helps to dispel the negative energy around the fear rather than leaving these fears in a dark corner of our mind.

3. Go around the group and name different events in our lives that are typically grieved.

- As a group give examples of when some well-meaning family member or friend grew impatient with your grieving, or said something hurtful because they could not identify with the grieving process. Discuss how that made you feel.
- Break into groups of two or three and take turns discussing a time in life you were unable to sufficiently grieve a loss. Identify what you think the consequences were for the inability to process that loss.
- Identify what action taken now might enable the completion of that unresolved grieving.
- Break into new groups of two or three and take turns discussing the most significant or recent event that has caused grief and share what this has been like.

4. In a group setting, discuss what has been the most difficult for you to adjust to in the past five years? In the past 10 years?

- Break into groups of two and further identify and explore what milestone or significant change in your life (regardless of your current age) has seemed momentous? Have you fully recovered from that change? What significance did it mean for the remainder of your life since it occurred?

5. Take a piece of paper and write the numbers down a left column of 1 through 6. At each number, write an accomplishment you have achieved to date. Choose one of these accomplishments. In groups of two, take turns discussing your particular accomplishment in

depth. Then have Partner No. 1, **close their eyes** and let Partner No. 2 **slowly** talk through the following visualization:

- "In a statement out loud, recall the event or reward you selected to revisit? Visualize yourself at the time.

- How did it made you feel?

- Let yourself feel the pride and satisfaction.

- Imagine now those who were around you, complementing you on your achievement, smiling, patting you on the back, shaking your hand, or giving you a hug.

- One by one, recognizing fully who they are, look them in the eye and let yourself take in their genuine congratulations and well-wishing.

- Is there anyone who could not be there whose absence saddened you?

- Identify who you would have wanted present that was not. Imagine facing them, now let them convey... to your mind's eye... how pleased they are with you.

- Let yourself be embraced by that genuine feeling.

- Let yourself feel pride. Let yourself feel loved.

- See yourself smiling, and let your heart feel great contentment.

- Take your time and when you are fully ready, slowly open your eyes."

———————————

- If you like, you can share your experience with your partner.

- If you wish to keep the experience to yourself, open your journal and make some notes about the experience, how you felt, who you saw and how you benefited from the exercise.

Allow some time within the full group setting to discuss specific questions or concerns pertaining to this chapter.

Chapter 6... Taking Care of Business

1. As a group:

- Discuss why people are generally hesitant to write a will.

- Discuss why people put off determining Guardians for their dependent children and making that decision legal. Discuss the possible danger and conflict of not having indicated such information legally.

- Discuss the necessity for having signed HIPAA forms for each physician, listing your spouse's name, or name(s) of your grown children, trusted friend, or health advocate.

2. Discuss the difference between a Last Will and Testament, A Living Trust and A Living Will. (These are defined in more detail in *Celebrate With Me: A Guide For Family and Friends At My Life's End.*)

- As a group, discuss various experiences or knowledge of Hospice, Compassion and Choices or other Palliative Care services due to a friend or family member utilizing these services.

- As a group, discuss the pros and cons of having a spouse or close friend as the designated health care agent. Why is it so important that the spouse or designated agent be fully aware if a DNR order or form is in place, and what actually takes place if 911 and paramedics are called at the last minute?

3. In groups of four, write a sample scenario of talking to a family member about decision making.

- Have two people write the scenario for the parent wishing to discuss the topics and decisions for their end-of-life at the reluctance of their child(ren).

- Have the other two members of the group write a sample scenario for the children who wish to discuss the relevant decision making with the reluctant parent(s).

- When these are prepared, take turns reading these among the full group. Compare and discuss the different ideas.

Allow some time within the full group setting to discuss specific questions or concerns pertaining to this chapter.

Chapter 7... What Am I Waiting for?

1. Individually consider if there is there something you might honestly admit to using as an escape from your life? Examples given in Chapter 7 were alcohol, sleep, food, or work.

- What forms of escape do you resort to when you are excessively stressed or needing to "get away?"

- Is this a healthy resort for you?

- Are there repercussions to your health or relationships by choosing this form of escape? Is there a better way to handle your stress?

2. Can you recall a parent or loved one ever expressing something they always wanted to do, but were unable to accomplish in their lifetime?

3. In groups of two, identify three or four things you have always want to do, but have not yet been able to for reasons of time, money, inconvenience, or priority.

- Jot down these three or four things and write the reason this goal has not been completed to date. It could be something you have always wanted to do, travel to, teach or take a course, or volunteer at a remote location. Don't be limited by your rational mind telling you it can never happen. Write it down.

- Take one of these items and write it into a statement of intent. Include What, When, Where, Who and How in your sentence. Example: "I want to travel to the coast of Italy before the end of 2011 with the love of my life. I want to fly into Florence and drive to the coast where we will stay in a villa for a week."

- After you have written your intention, copy this statement(s) on sticky notes and place these on your bathroom mirror, in your day-timer, on the dash of your car, and any place else you will see it daily.

- Visualize yourself doing this when you get up in the morning, and before retiring for sleep at night. Don't let the idea go away. Don't succumb to the negativity of your rational mind. Keep it close to your heart and watch the possibilities unfold.

- Take turns reading your statement to your group partner.

- See yourself actually doing this goal in your mind's eye. Feel your excitement at the prospect of doing it as you describe the sensations of what this will be like for you.

5. As a group, discuss what the word "passion" means to you? Are you living your life with passion? It is a word not frequently used except in the concept of being "passionate" with someone. What in your life are you passionate about? Discuss these examples among the group.

6. Allow time in the group setting to discuss a "purposeful life." Ask yourself if you are living a life with an identified purpose. Have you already accomplished an identified purpose in your life?

- Discuss these questions and your answers with a partner in the group.

- Following this discussion with the partner, quickly ask each other, "Who are you waiting for to give you permission to live your life more fully?" What is the first thing which comes to mind? Is there a person or situation which actually comes to mind when answering this question? Make a note of your answer and journal on this question further.

Allow some time within the full group setting to discuss specific questions or concerns pertaining to this chapter.

Chapter 8... Community and Remembrances

1. As a group, have each member quickly write down the first six words that come to mind when asked to "pick the six words which you think define you."

- Then have each group member take an 8 ½ by 11 inch plain paper and holding it vertically, write the six words in large letters across the page, filling the majority of the page with the six words.

- With a safety pin or tape, have each member attach the paper to the front of their shirt.

- Have everyone get up and walk around the room pairing up to ask each other about only one of the words listed.

- Each pair will take a turn choosing one word from the other's list, and ask why they chose that word, or "tell me about how _____ describes you?"

- Place an "X" next to the word now discussed.

- After each has discussed one word on their paper, find a new partner and repeat the process for as long as time allows. You may not get through the entire list.

- Have all the participants sit down again. Ask the participants to now review their six words again, and ask them to change any word for another that they now think better describes them. If time allows, ask them to find a partner and now share the words they changed and why.

2. As a group allow a few minutes to think of a friend or family member whose stories bring back fond memories. These might be funny stories told about this particular friend or family member in remembrance.

- Allow some time to let a few people briefly share with the group these remembrances.

- Then allow a few moments for each member to individually write a paragraph, a story, which they would love remembered about them.

3. Our "community" may not be a group of people who know each other. Our community may consist of people spread out all over the country with who we are still in contact, with which we have had history, shared emotions and made memories together. These are the people who have contributed to the patch quilt we have created that is our life.

Take a few minutes now and jot down the names of these important people in your life who are or have been a part of your community.

4. Now list those in your most immediate or local "community." Do you nurture your relationship with these people? Are they people you see or who remain in contact with you? Who among

these are due to hear from you? Let them know you care and wish to stay in contact.

Allow some time within the full group setting to discuss specific questions or concerns pertaining to this chapter.

Chapter 9... Transformation

1. Discuss the meaning of transformation, and then engage sharing as a group what that experience seemed like for those who have witnessed the passing of a loved one.

2. Letting imaginations run free, encourage the group to entertain what it might be like after death. If time allows, use paper and a color medium for greater freedom of expression. Explore possibilities without rational limitation.

3. Encourage members to journal on the following statement: "If I could plan for this important transition — in any way influencing reality with my preferences for what the experience would be like… the following are my sincere thoughts on how I would wish this transition to take place."

4. In groups of two, discuss how you would prioritize the remainder of your life if you learned today that you have only three months left to live. Make individual lists of important things you would wish to do, and the people you would want to spend more time with during that time.

5. As a group discuss what comes to mind when asked, "What legacy are you leaving those you will some day leave behind?"

6. As a group, plan a *Celebration Of Life*, honoring each group participant. Be sure that ideas for this celebration are a collaboration representing each group member. This might be an occasion for people to bring in celebratory food, decorations, favorite and meaningful photos, and possibly invite family members and friends.

7. It is further encouraged that a similar party be given by each group participant at some point before the end of their life, remembering

and inviting significant people in their life to share in stories, remembrances, gratitude and celebration. List now the people in your life you would want invited to attend your celebration.

8. Going back over this list of guests, what would you like to say to each individual in a way of thanking them for being in your life?

9. As a group, discuss the most valuable aspects of this Group Discussion study. What has been the most helpful information from the book chapters? What has this process revealed about yourself that you didn't expect?

Allow some time within the full group setting to discuss specific questions or concerns pertaining to this chapter.

Comments by group discussion participants after completing the questions and discussions on the book chapters:

"Completing the group discussion exercises reminded me to live each day fully, to take care of any unfinished business with loved ones now, and to appreciate myself and others more."

"Sharing my thoughts and feelings with others in a group setting encouraged me to actually work through my fears, and address my wishes regarding my own death. Because I felt safe in our church group, I was able to participate in discussions and voice my most personal thoughts about death. I have never been able to discuss these topics with anyone else before."

"I now feel lighter about my thoughts concerning death. Taking part in a group to discuss *Please Dance At My Funeral*, and share in the exercises together, helps me feel more in control, and outlines what I need to do now so my wishes are documented."

"You need to really participate with an open mind to get the most out of a discussion group on this topic. The exercises and homework journaling are so important. When you examine your thoughts honestly, the answers are very revealing and provoking."

"I came away from the discussion group with the vital reminder that life is short. I'm forty, and healthy, but the book questions have motivated me to do what I need to do, say what I need to say *now* — and to forgive, and let go, and love."

"The discussions about this book remind and inspire me that I need to celebrate this life *now*."

Role Play Demonstration Script

*A One Act Play Demonstrating An Approach To
Initiate Communication Regarding Advance Directives*

"MY FINAL WORDS"

Written by Judith Haynes

MOTHER'S KITCHEN: Middle-aged daughter visiting her mother; helping with dishes when beginning conversation.

DAUGHTER: "Mom, my friend, Lynn... (hesitation) ...well, ...her mother died last week."Mother curiously glances over at daughter but waits for her to say more.

DAUGHTER: "She seemed fine and then all of a sudden had some pain and went into the hospital."

MOTHER: (Seeming distant, turning away from daughter, dismissing wanting to continue the subject.) "Oh? She must have been a much older woman." (Sets bowl on counter and moves to sit in chair at table; taking towel with her.)

DAUGHTER: (Drying off her hands and moving where she can see her mother's face while leaning against counter.) "No, Mom. She was only 69. She had seemed fine. No symptoms to speak of. But once she got into the hospital, she went into a coma, and was on life support for nine days!"

MOTHER: (Looking up into space, not at daughter while contemplating, then softly repeated.) "...only 69?" (voice trails off) "...I'm only ...."

DAUGHTER: (Sits down opposite mother at table but now facing her, continues.) "Mom, the thing is, there was no previous conversation with Lynn's mom about her health, or what if she ever went into the hospital, or what if she was in "Intensive Care." Lynn's brother and sisters didn't know what to do. None of them knew what their mother would have wanted. And now, they don't know how they are going to pay for her hospital bills!" :

MOTHER: (Looking up at her daughter in surprise.) "Pay for her hospital bills!? Their mother just died, and all they can think about is money?" (Looks away in disgust, shaking head.)

DAUGHTER: (Continuing, facing mother's face.) "That's just it, Mom. They don't even have a chance to properly grieve because they are now consumed with selling everything to try to pay for the expenses! No one had any idea what it was going to cost for all the days their mother was in a coma! The cost comes to thousands of dollars, and Lynn doesn't know how she and her husband can help with their share and still afford to send their son to college next year!"

MOTHER: (Tossing her nose in the air and diverting her eyes away from daughter.) "Oh. Well, …they should have planned better! Are they poor?"

DAUGHTER: (Leaning or moving slightly to again have eye contact with her mother.) "No, Mom. Just average people like us, with average medical coverage. Lynn said that someone in the billing department at the hospital told her almost 50 million American's don't have insurance. They just can't afford it any more. But lots of people. (Pause, looking up to remember a number) …I think she said almost 40 percent of people admitted to the hospital end up in the intensive care unit at the end, like Lynn's mother. And that's what costs so much. (Looking away, thinking of own possibilities.) A person could loose everything just trying to do every medical miracle known to modern man to save the person they love from ever dying."

MOTHER: (Brushing crumbs off her apron with the towel in her hand, throwing her head back and chuckling before speaking.) "I remember your Uncle Roy thinking for sure he was going to die right in the waiting room! It seemed like he was waiting a long time to get care when he nearly had a heart attack. To this day he swears he could smell pizza—and there he lay in pain. (Her voice trails off remembering and shaking her head.) ...could hardly breathe ...he kept smelling pizza...."

DAUGHTER: (Quickly turning her gaze now back to mother.) "But that's just it, Mom. If that happened to you, I don't know what you'd want me to do either?"

MOTHER: (Looking up surprised, then indignant.) "Well! You just don't have to worry! I don't plan on kicking the bucket any time soon! So we can just stop talking about it!"

DAUGHTER: (Placing a hand on her mother's hand.) "No, Mom. Lynn's mom didn't plan on dying when she did either. That's just it. The time just isn't something we can plan. But there is something we can do."

DAUGHTER: (Gets up from the table and goes to her purse; pulls some papers from her purse and returns to the table. Places papers gently down in front of mother and continues.) "Mom... at the hospital some people talked to Lynn's family about what they call "medical directives." (Looking into her mother's eyes, continues.) "Mom, I got a set of these forms, and it would give me real peace of mind to know what you would want me to do if we were in that situation."

MOTHER: (Mother looks up at daughters face with eyes wide but not speaking; ...then looks down at forms on table.)

DAUGHTER: (Putting her hand on her mother's arm, looks into her Mother's eyes.) "Mom, I wouldn't want to live the rest of my life knowing the decisions I had to make might not be what you would want. Can we please look at these together?" (She moves her chair closer to her Mother's chair and begins to turn the first page of the forms.)

Buscaglia, Leo, *Living, Loving & Learning*, New Jersey, Charles B. Slack, Inc. 1982.

Chödrön, Pema, *The Wisdom of No Escape* Shambhala Publications, Boston, Mass. 1991.

Cousins, Norman, *Anatomy of an Ilness As Perceived by the Patient: Reflections on Healing and Regeneration*, Bantam, Boston, Mass. 1979.

Elliott, Grace Loucks, *"Death is inextricably woven ..."To Come Full Circle: Towards an Understanding of Death*, Industrial Media Services 1972.

Ghandi, M., *"There Would be nothing to frighten you..."*, Source/date unknown.

Goethe, *"Nothing is worth more than this day."* Source/date unknown.

Guardaldi, Vince, *Linus and Lucy* (Song), 1964.

Huxley, Aldous, (1894-1963) British Writer/Philosopher *"A Childlike man is not a man whose development has been arrested;..."*

The Gospel to Thomas, *"If you bring forth that which you have within you..."* (Jesus's as recorded by Didymos Judas Thomas) from The Nag Hammadi Library.

Jones, J. Phillips, *Light on Death: The Spiritual Art of Dying,* (Page 81) China, Palace Press International, 2007.

Klein, Mark, *Serendipity* (Movie) Released October 2001.

Lincoln, Abraham, American, 16th U.S. President, (1809-1865).

Luke 8:17, (Quoting Jesus) *"Nothing is hidden that will not become evident;..."* The Holy Bible.

Maudsley, Henry, *"The sorrow which has no vent in tears..."* English Physiologist, 1935-1918, *Pathology of Mind,* 1879.

Mullins, Rich, *"We Walk By Faith and Not By Sight..."* Event, location and date unknown.

Powell, John Enoch, *"If my ship sails from sight,..."* 1912-1998 British writer. Source and date unknown.

Pravervand, Pierre, *"To bless means to wish, unconditionally..."* The *Gentle Art of Blessing,* Atria Books, 2009.

Schultz, Charles M., *A Charlie Brown Christmas* (TV Movie) 1965.

Schweitzer, Albert, German medical Missionary, Theologian, Musician and Philosopher. 1952 Nobel Peace Prize, (1875-1965).

Shaffer, Carolyn R., & Kristin Anundsen, *"Some people think they are in community..."* by David Spangler (Page 157) and *"The process of really being with other people in a safe,... "* by Bill Kauth (Page 72). *Creating Community Anywhere: Finding Support and Connection In A Fragmented World,* (Tarcher/Putnam, 1993; reissued by CCC Press, 2005).

Smedes, Lewis B., *Forgive & Forget: Healing the Hurts We Don't Deserve,* Harper One, 2007.

Thoele, Sue Patton, *"Deep listening is miraculous for both listener..."* The *Woman's Book Of Soul,* Conari Press, 2000.

Wells, Ann, *"A Story To Live By,"* L.A. Times, May 27, 1998.

Wilson, Woodrow T., American, 28th US President, (1856-1924).

Zola, Emile, French Novelist, Critic and Activist 1840-1902, *"If you ask me what I came to do in this world,..."*

Advance Medical Directive: A form used to make your final wishes for your medical care known to your family and medical care providers. Generally, when you are at the end of your life and are incapacitated when admitted to the hospital, your decisions indicated on this form cover what treatment you want to receive, and what treatment you wish to refuse. If you are able to do so, you can still change your mind regarding treatment once admitted.

Altruistic Being: That which identifies with a higher awareness to selflessness; devotion to the welfare of others.

Authentic Self: A sacred, natural state of being; being genuinely you.

Compassion and Choices: Compassion & Choices supports, educates and advocates for choice and care at the end of life, committed to maximizing the options for a good death, including improving pain and palliative care, enforcing living wills and advance directives, and legalizing aid in dying.

Consciousness: Consciousness is an expression of higher awareness of the essential self.

Durable Power of Attorney: Similar to the Power of Attorney, only this designation allows the agent under the POA to continue to act on your behalf, in your best interest, even after you are declared incompetent or become incapacitated.

Energy: Energy is the base of all that exists, seen or unseen, in the Universe.

Frequency: Everything which exists, whether an idea, an emotion, thought or word, has a frequency. Every organism, cell and atom exist as energy and each has a level of vibration or frequency.

HIPAA: The HIPAA Privacy Law provides federal protections for personal health information held by covered entities and gives patients an array of rights with respect to that information. At the same time, it permits the disclosure of personal health information needed for patient care and other important purposes. This protection specifies a series of administrative, physical, and technical safeguards for covered entities to use to assure the confidentiality, integrity, and availability of protected health information.

Hospice: An organization offering comfort care for the dying when medical treatment is no longer expected to cure the disease or prolong life. Hospice is provided where the person resides. The term may also apply to an insurance benefit that pays the costs of comfort care (usually at home) for patients with a prognosis of six months or less. Hospice emphasizes palliative rather than curative treatment; quality rather than quantity of life. Professional medical care is given, and sophisticated symptom relief provided. The patient and family are both included in the care plan and emotional, spiritual and practical support is given based on the patient's wishes and family's needs.

Intensive Care Unit: A part of the hospital which accommodates a patient designated as needing specific life saving services provided by equipment which include a mechanical ventilator to assist breathing through a tube or a tracheotomy opening; cardiac monitors including external pacemakers, and defibrillators; dialysis equipment for renal problems; equipment for the constant monitoring of bodily functions; a web of intravenous lines, feeding tubes, suction pumps, drains and catheters; and a wide array of drugs to treat the main condition(s). Medically induced comas, analgesics, and induced sedation reduce pain and prevent secondary infections.

Last Will and Testament: A will or testament, a legal declaration by which a person names one or more persons to manage his estate and provides for the transfer of his property at death.

Living Trust: A Will substitute, can provide your assets if you become disabled, can avoid probate upon your death, can protect your children while still providing for a spouse, maintains privacy for your estate plan and financial affairs, save money in estate taxes versus that of a simple Will, but generally cost more to set up; and definitely needs the skills of an experienced attorney to draft.

Living Will: A living will is a document which applies to the final moments of life.

Palliative Care: Patient and family focused care to optimize the quality of life, reducing suffering at the end-of-life, while addressing the physical, emotional, social and spiritual needs.

Power of Attorney (POA): is a document designating an agent or attorney-in-fact, who is both trustworthy and knowledgeable, to act strictly for your benefit, and has the power to pay bills, cash checks, withdraw money, trade stock and sign deeds that is in your best interest for the period of time while you are incapacitated. See Durable Power of Attorney. A POA document cannot substitute for a Will or Trust, and becomes void upon your death—your agent cannot further act for you or represent your estate.

Resonance: Resonance occurs when successive impulses are applied to a vibrating object in time with its natural frequency resulting in increased amplitude; such as in sound waves, or the movement of swinging; our subtle energy in synchronicity with that of others, of our immediate environment, and that of the world and Universe.

Soul: The Soul is the permanent, essential self; the essence of the energy and frequency greater than the physical embodiment. The essential core is integrated with the physical embodiment, and capable of a greater and Universal wisdom.

Transcendence: The process of changing beyond the limitations of the physical being, independent of the material world.

Transformation: Transformation occurs when there is a change in form, behavior and structure without changing the essence of the being.

Transition: Transition is the "in-between" process where there is reorganization of consciousness, and energetic changes taking place.

This process is a subtle change when awareness is expanding and eventually develops toward transformation.

Vibration: Vibration is the stimulation of a frequency, determined by the length of a wave, which can broadcast frequency or value of frequency as a signal. Music, colors, sound and words are all forms of vibrational energy.

Author Biography

Meet Judith Haynes...

Judith Haynes is an N.D., a Naturopath, promoting natural ways to achieve better health for nearly three decades. Her enthusiasm for helping people comes from her own experience with a natural approach to healing that saved her life almost twenty years ago. Helping clients to maintain health and wellness naturally includes discussions about loss, and eventual end-of-life, whether pertaining to the client, or to the client's family members.

Judith is devoted to educating, and speaking on ways to empower people regarding their health and their lives. This book is a product of her desire to bring about an easy to read guide which presents end-of-life topics in an informative way. Judith's intention is to present the idea of conscious dying, while encouraging us to more fully live our lives now.

Over the last 30 years, Judith has taught various courses, and given lectures about health and motivational topics—most recently including *Keys to Your Empowerment: How To Be In The Driver's Seat In Your Life!* Judith is a mother, grandmother, speaker and author who has always questioned, sought truth, and encouraged others to join her in stretching our minds beyond imagined limits.

Alzheimer's Association
National Headquarters
225 N. Michigan Ave.
17th Floor
Chicago, IL 60601
1-800-272-3900
www.alz.org

American Bar Association
321 N. Clark St.
Chicago, IL 60654
1-800-285-2221
www.aba.org

American Cancer Society
National Home Office
250 Williams St.
Atlanta, GA 30303
1-800-227-2345
www.cancer.org

American Hospice Foundation
2120 L Street, N.W., Suite 200
Washington, DC 20037
(202) 223-0204
1-800-347-1413
www.americanhospice.org

Compassion and Choices
P. O. Box 101810
Denver, Colorado 80250
1-800-247-7421
www.compassionandchoices.org

National Academy of
Elder Law Attorneys
1577 Spring Hill Road, Ste. 220
Vienna, VA 22182
(703) 942-5711
www.naela.org

National Association of Home
Care and Hospice
228 7 Street, S.E.
Washington, DC 20003
(202) 546-4759
www.nahc.org

National Hospice Organization
1901 N. Moore St., Suite 901
Arlington, VA 22209
1-800-658-8898
(703) 243-5900
www.caringinfo.org

National Hospice & Palliative
Care Organization
1731 King Street, Suite 100
Alexandria, Virginia 22314
703/837-1500
703/837-1233 (fax)
www.nhpco.org

Judith Haynes is available to speak at seminars, conferences, and organizations. If you would like to discuss a possible speaking engagement or to obtain additional copies of this book, please contact us:

A Celebration of Life Publishing
P. O. Box 631494, Highlands Ranch, Colorado 80163-1494
303-619-1727
www.JudithHaynes.com